Tony Jacklin
YOUR GAME AND MINE

Tony Jacklin
YOUR GAME AND MINE

Bill Robertson

SACKVILLE
BOOKS

First published in 1990
by Sackville Books Ltd
Stradbroke, Suffolk, England

© Teeshots Services Ltd and Sackville Books Ltd

Designed and produced by Sackville Design Group Ltd
Art director: Al Rockall
Editor: Heather Thomas
Photographs: Matthew Harris
Typesetting: Jean Cussons

British Library Cataloguing in Publication Data
Jacklin, Tony 1944 -
   Your game and mine
  1 Golf. Techniques
  I. Title   II. Robertson, Bill
  796. 3523

  ISBN 0-948615-42-7

Printed and bound in Spain by Graficas Estella, S.A. Navarra

Contents

Foreword

The art of the professional, regardless of the sport, is the ability to make the game look easy. Golf is the perfect example where the top players, those who are constantly on the leader boards, have a simple and straightforward action. The apparent ease of action which gains them both distance and accuracy is built upon solid foundations, reliable basics which form the cornerstone of the most talked about aspect of golf, the swing.

Your Game and Mine is intended to help the improving player, to direct the golfer towards a lower handicap by means of a higher appreciation of the basics of the game. The game must be kept simple and that must start with the swing itself. There is no need for a wasted search for a complicated swing which will be impossible to reproduce on a regular basis. In my opinion, the key to success in the golf game is simplicity which, with care and attention to detail, can be counted to serve you well wherever and whenever you play golf.

The improving player must be able to rely on basics each and every time the course is challenged, with the key areas of the game mastered to the extent that they become a routine that is natural. That routine preparation for each and every shot should be built around the important aspects that no golfer can afford to forget.

The stance, alignment, grip, ball position and swing should, as a matter of course, form a mental checklist that will serve all players well over the duration of their golf careers. Improving players will continue to meet with success if they can maintain faith in those key areas, using them with care and precision in the pre-strike routine.

The other important factor is control. Without control the golfer will, more often than not, return to the clubhouse a dejected player with the scorecard reflecting the lack of control. It is vital that you play within the bounds of total control and never hit flat out.

Your Game and Mine is intended to focus your mind on the simple aspects of the game of golf. It is, essentially, a simple game and therefore there is no great need to complicate the issue. Build the key areas I use myself into your game and it will be stronger and, hopefully, more enjoyable.

Good luck.

Tony Jacklin.

Introduction
by Bill Robertson

Several years ago, I was asked to write an article, describing the best three shots that I had ever seen played in the final round of the British Open Championship. The only criteria for inclusion was that the shot in question must have played a significant part in the eventual outcome of the Championship.

In third place I chose that marvellous seven iron approach shot played by Tom Watson to the final hole, in his epic head-to-head battle with Jack Nicklaus in the final round of the 1977 Open Championship at Turnberry.

Second place went to that great golfer Gary Player for an unbelievable three wood second shot to the par five 14th hole at Carnoustie on the last day of the 1968 Open. Player, who was leading his playing partner Jack Nicklaus by a slender margin, had the Golden Bear breathing down his neck but was still able to produce that memorable three wood which came to rest within three feet of the hole.

My first choice, however, went unquestionably to the drive hit by Tony Jacklin at the 72nd hole of the 1969 Open Championship at Royal Lytham and St Annes. Even to this day, I can't recall a better shot ever in a crunch situation in a major tournament.

It had been over twenty years since a British golfer had held aloft that famous old claret jug and there was a tremendous air of expectancy and excitement among the thousands of spectators who flocked to follow Tony's progress on the last day. And when

Tony set out on the final round, he was carrying not just his own hopes and aspirations but also those of the home fans, desperate to acclaim a British winner.

Tony stood up to the pressure of that last day magnificently, and when he eventually reached the 18th hole, he still held a slender two shot lead over his nearest rival and playing partner, New Zealander Bob Charles.

Throughout the drama and tension of that final round, Tony had somehow been able to retain both his rhythm and composure and that coveted title was now within his grasp. However, the 18th hole at Royal Lytham is one of the toughest closing holes in championship golf and the tee shot one of the most demanding. Charles drove first and although his ball ran into the rough, the lie was good and he would have no difficulty reaching the green with his second shot.

Facing a man considered by many to be the best putter in the world, Tony was only too well aware that the Championship was far from over and that he could not afford a slip at this crucial stage. And as the huge gallery following the final pair fell silent, I can still recall the TV commentator whispering, "Come on, Tony, just one more good drive" as Tony stepped up to play the most important shot of his golfing career.

It was the ultimate test of both nerve and technique but, as history records, Tony passed with flying colours, splitting the fairway

Tony Jacklin holds the Open Championship trophy aloft after his victory at Royal Lytham in July 1969. This was an historic occasion — the first time an English golfer had won since Max Faulkner in 1951.

with the best drive seen at the 18th hole, not just on the final day, but throughout the whole of the Championship.

Confidence in his ability and a positive attitude to the game are two qualities that Tony Jacklin has always had in abundance throughout his career as a professional golfer; coupled with that touch or arrogance that is inherent to the make-up of all the great sportsmen. And those qualities were displayed for all to see in that one stunning shot.

An equally positive seven iron approach, followed by two putts, clinched an historical victory for Tony Jacklin and also signalled to the world that, after so many years in the wings, Britain once again had a golfer capable of holding centre stage.

And just to prove the point, Jacklin crossed the Atlantic the following year and became the first British golfer to capture the US Open title since Ted Ray in 1920. This remarkable Open double served not only to confirm Tony's status as a world-class player, but it also proved the inspiration for those Europeans who were to follow — men such as Seve Ballesteros, Sandy Lyle, Bernhard Langer and Nick Faldo.

Tony Jacklin also brought the same attitudes and beliefs that he held as a player to the Ryder Cup captaincy. His playing record certainly earned him the respect of the 1983 European Ryder Cup team: he'd been there, felt the tension and understood the pressures of playing not for himself, but for his country. For in the same year that he became Open champion, Tony also played out an enthralling final act in the Ryder Cup matches at Royal Birkdale when he halved the last singles match with the great Jack Nicklaus to ensure that the series finished with honours even.

However, Tony brought more than just his reputation as a world-class golfer to the team. He also instilled a genuine belief among the players that they were every bit as good as their American counterparts. And for the first time in many years, players who had previously felt that they were there only to make up the numbers, really believed that they had a genuine chance at last of winning on American soil.

In his years of battling almost single-handed against the Americans in their own backyard, Tony had learned many hard but valuable lessons. And he put the experience he had gained playing on the American PGA Tour to good use, as he planned his strategy for the 1983 Ryder Cup matches at the PGA National Club in Florida. No longer would the Europeans arrive in the United States feeling like the underdogs. Tony insisted that everything about the team's preparation should be to the highest standards, and that included chartering Concorde for the flight to America.

The preparation for the match was meticulous and nothing was left to chance. Tony spent long hours with the team members, getting to know their likes and dislikes, discovering their strengths and weaknesses and, above all, ensuring that the pairings that he chose would blend well on the course. Off the course, their every need was catered for; the team members were made to feel that they were special and, in return, they gave their all for their captain.

On this occasion, however, the European team were pipped at the post, losing by the narrowest of margins in a nail-biting climax on the final day. However, the closeness of the contest underlined the fact that American domination of the event could no longer be taken for granted, and two years later, when the teams met at The Belfry in England, there were high hopes of a European victory.

Tony knew how close his team had come to winning in Florida and was quietly confident that with the support of a home gallery, the European team would be able to turn the tables on the Americans. And so it proved, with Tony's leadership qualities once again coming to the fore, as he inspired the European team to an historic victory. But perhaps the pinnacle of Tony's reign as Ryder Cup

*Tony Jacklin savours his moment
of glory after leading the
European team to victory in the
1987 Ryder Cup at Muirfield
Village, Ohio.*

captain came in 1987 when the European team beat the Americans on their home soil for the first time in the fifty-year history of the event.

Retaining the trophy when the matches returned to The Belfry in 1989, gave Europe a unique Ryder Cup hat-trick and made Tony Jacklin the most successful captain ever. It was at this point, after eight years in the hot seat, that Tony decided to step down as captain in order to concentrate on other aspects of his career, secure in the knowledge that Bernard Gallacher, the man elected to take over as captain, would continue to build on the foundations he had laid down.

Although officially retired from serious tournament golf, Tony is still actively involved in the game. A popular TV commentator on both sides of the Atlantic, he is currently engaged in several golf course design and construction projects. There is also great demand for his knowledge of the golf swing at golf clinics all over the world, and he has recently completed a series of instructional videos.

Throughout his playing career, Tony retained a smooth, rhythmic swing that was the envy of many of his fellow tournament professionals, and which characterized his game, even when playing under the most intense pressure. During a career in professional golf which began as a sixteen-year-old assistant at Potters Bar golf club in Hertfordshire, England, and carried him to the very pinnacle of the game as a double Open Championship winner, Tony Jacklin has stayed true to two important swing principles. The first is: 'Keep it simple'; and the second is: 'Always play within yourself'.

To gather material for this book I spent some time with Tony at his home in Spain, where we talked at length about many different aspects of the game, including these two important swing principles. During my visit I also played golf with Tony at the spectacular new San Roque Club where he is Director of Golf, and during the round, he demonstrated

how to cure many of the faults that plague the weekend golfer.

Tony Jacklin has a straightforward, no-nonsense approach to golf instruction which I'm sure you will find both refreshing and easy to understand, and he also passes on some sound advice on golf equipment.

Watching Tony Jacklin play, it was difficult to imagine that some twenty years had passed since he won the Open Championship. His swing looked every bit as smooth and effortless as it did when he hit that memorable drive straight down the centre of the 18th fairway at Royal Lytham, which is surely the best possible testament to those two swing principles: keep it simple and play within yourself.

*Tony Jacklin hugs the trophy as he
celebrates the European team's retention of the
Ryder Cup at The Belfry in 1989.*

The fundamentals of golf

If I was asked to choose one thing that I feel has contributed most to my success as a professional golfer, it would be confidence. Even before those twelve magical months between July 1969 and June 1970 when I won both the British and US Open championships, I was certain that I had the ability to compete and win at the very highest level of the game. However, although confidence is certainly an asset, it takes a great deal more than just belief in your ability to become a winner. It also requires dedication, commitment, a burning desire to be the best and, perhaps most important of all, a sound knowledge of the fundamentals of the golf swing.

These fundamentals are the basic building blocks from which every golfer develops his or her swing. And by the same token, they also provide the answers to most of the faults which from time to time creep into everyone's game — from superstar to rabbit. No matter how much natural talent you may have, or how dedicated you are to becoming a good golfer, without a sound knowledge of the basic fundamentals of the swing, progress will, at best, be painfully slow. Therefore if you are a comparative newcomer to golf, learning to understand the basic fundamentals of the swing will provide the tools with which you can start to build a sound one. And even if you have played the game for some time, reviewing the swing fundamentals is an exercise that every golfer, regardless of ability, should undertake on a regular basis.

Posture

If you are uncomfortable as you address the ball the chances are that you will hit a poor shot. At address, you should be well balanced with your weight evenly distributed. The body should feel supple in order to help start the swing smoothly.

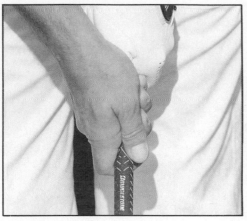

The grip

The correct grip is one of the most important factors in developing a good swing. This is because the hands are not only the link between the body and the club, but they also control the clubface. Newcomers to the game may find gripping the club correctly a little awkward at first. However, this will pass and they will reap the rewards that come from a sound grip.

Alignment

No matter how good your posture, or how well you grip the golf club, you will never be able to hit straight shots consistently unless you learn to aim your body correctly. As a high percentage of fairways missed result from poor alignment, it is essential that you develop a reliable method of aiming both the club and your body in the right direction.

Ball position

To a great extent, playing good golf is about being able to repeat a series of actions in the proper sequence, time after time after time. It is equally important that the culmination of these actions results in the clubhead making contact with the ball at precisely the right time and place, making it essential that you establish the correct ball position for every shot.

Swing plane

To enable the clubhead to strike the ball squarely and at the correct angle, it is important that the hands, arms and shoulders all work together within the same plane. Everyone has their own natural swing plane which is determined mainly by height. Learning how to swing within the correct plane is essential if you want to hit good golf shots.

The fundamentals of golf

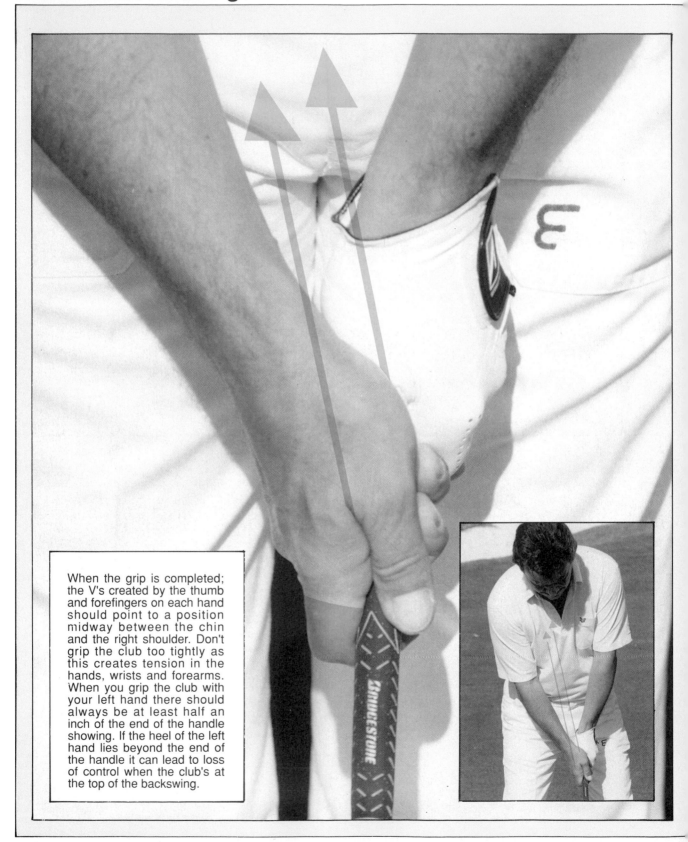

When the grip is completed; the V's created by the thumb and forefingers on each hand should point to a position midway between the chin and the right shoulder. Don't grip the club too tightly as this creates tension in the hands, wrists and forearms. When you grip the club with your left hand there should always be at least half an inch of the end of the handle showing. If the heel of the left hand lies beyond the end of the handle it can lead to loss of control when the club's at the top of the backswing.

How I build my grip

Within a framework of the basic fundamentals of the golf swing everyone develops their own individual method of hitting the ball. If you get the opportunity to watch the top professionals in action, you'll be amazed at the variety of swings on view. However, although they may differ in their method of swinging the club, one thing that all top players have in common is a good grip.

There are three recognised ways of gripping the club; the Vardon, the Interlock and the Hammer, or Baseball, grips. Although the Vardon grip is the most common, like Jack Nicklaus, throughout my career I have always favoured the Interlock grip. This is because I don't have particularly large hands and I feel that the Interlock helps me hold the club more securely. Regardless of which grip you favour, the main thing is to ensure that the hands work together and not as independent units. A poor grip is one of the main reasons for hitting wayward shots, and that's why it's worth taking time to check your grip before every shot

When building your grip, it's important to anchor the club securely in the left hand. This is done by gripping the handle firmly with the last three fingers of the hand, until it sits snugly in position, under the pad beneath the heel of your left hand, and the thumb is then positioned on top of the handle. The right hand is then applied to the handle, with the middle two fingers sliding up the grip until they are positioned against the forefinger of the left hand. With the Interlocking grip, the forefinger of the left hand is then entwined with the little finger of the right hand. Finally the thumb is positioned so that the soft pad of flesh under the base of the right thumb sits comfortably over the top of the left, with the end of the thumb also resting on top of the grip.

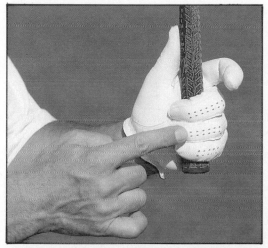

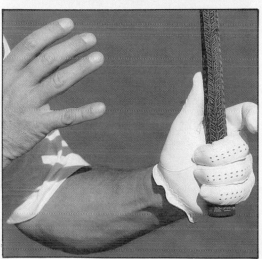

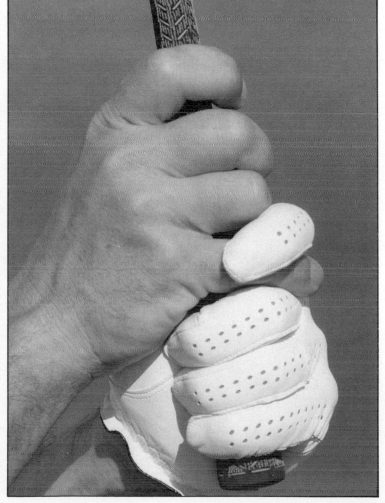

The fundamentals of golf

The Vardon grip

This is the most popular grip among modern-day golfers and the one favoured by the majority of tournament professionals. The procedure for taking up the Vardon grip is to all intents and purposes the same as the interlocking. However, instead of the little finger of the right hand intertwining with the forefinger of the left hand, it rests on the top of the index finger. There are some players and teachers who feel that the Vardon grip is slightly stronger than the interlocking because it allows the forefinger of the left hand to remain fully in contact with the handle of the club. Whatever grip you decide to adopt, it's important to remember that the position of the back of the left hand should mirror the position of the leading edge of the clubface. And try not to grip the club too tightly. It should be held mainly in the fingers with just enough pressure to keep control without creating any tension in the wrists or forearms.

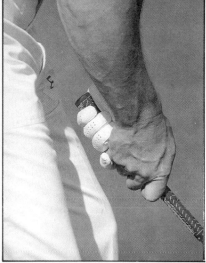

You should always leave at least half an inch of the butt of the club visible when taking up your grip.

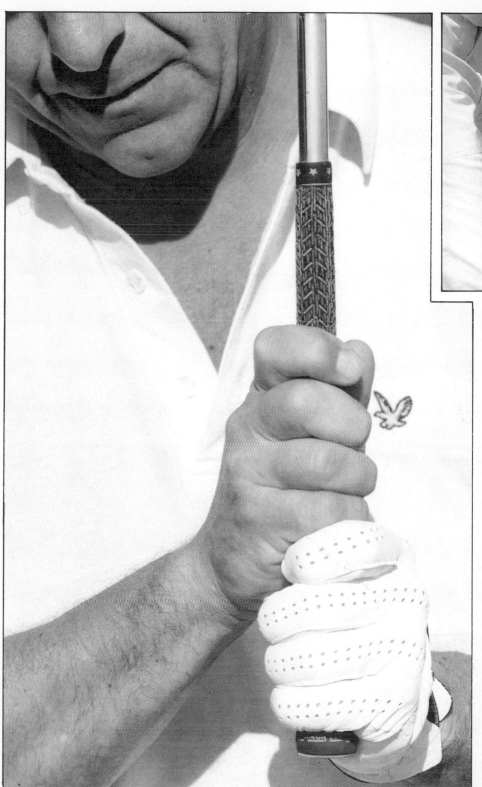

The Hammer/Baseball grip

This grip was used mainly in the early days of the game when the handles on clubs were much thicker than on present-day models and it was difficult to get the hands working close together. Because of this, all the fingers and thumbs were used when holding the club. This type of grip also helped to promote the active hand action required to achieve the best results from the old hickory shafted clubs. Some golfers with exceptionally small hands still use the Hammer, or Baseball, grip and the last professional to adopt this grip successfully was the late Dai Rees. The little Welshman was a regular tournament winner and Ryder Cup player and, pound for pound, one of the longest hitters of his era.

The fundamentals of golf

Common grip faults

If the grip is faulty, the golfer is then required to compensate in other areas of the swing, in an attempt to return the clubface square to the target line. This in turn tends to create further swing faults, all of which could have been avoided had he taken the time to check his grip. I can't stress too much the importance of checking your grip before every shot. When the butt end of the handle is not gripped correctly (opposite) and the club gets to the top of the backswing, control is lost, which makes it almost impossible to return the clubhead square to the target line. Gripping the club correctly (below) enables me to keep the club on line at the top of the backswing and increases my chances of hitting the shot on target.

Too strong

When the left hand is also placed on the handle in a strong position, the V's formed by the thumb and forefinger of both hands, point to a position outside the right shoulder, instead of midway between the head and the shoulder. This type of grip encourages the hands to turn rather than hinge, which causes the clubhead to return to the ball closed (facing to the left) and results in a hooked shot. Turning the hands too far to the left is a common fault among beginners. In an attempt to establish a powerful position from which to attack the ball, they are encouraged to grip the club more in the palm of the right hand than in the fingers. In some cases, they also position their right thumb behind the shaft.

Too weak

When the hands are positioned with the V's pointing directly at the chin, or even slightly further to the left, this is described as a weak grip. Because the hands are positioned too far to the left, the left arm will be out of position as it starts back from the ball. This has the effect of forcing the club to travel back outside the target line and, in an effort to gain strength, the left arm rotates to the left, opening the clubface. With a weak grip the hands are required to work much harder in an effort to square the clubface through natural rotation at impact. And if the hands fail to square the clubface and it remains open, the ball will slice to the right.

The fundamentals of golf

Watch a superstar like Nick Faldo or Seve Ballesteros preparing to hit a shot and you will quickly notice how much care and attention both men give to alignment. Almost every tournament professional, myself included, has a set routine designed to help aim both the body and the clubface in the right direction. For pros and weekend golfers alike, there is nothing more frustrating than to make a good pass at the ball, only to see it fly off in the wrong direction; not because of any fault in the actual swing, but as the result of poor alignment.

Alignment

Here is one step-by-step method of setting up that might help you hit straighter shots.

1 Before you set up to hit the shot, stand directly behind the ball and visualize the ball-to-target line. Then try to find a spot, such as an old tee peg or a mark of the turf that is directly on your ball-to-target line but much closer to the ball; it is far easier to line up on an object that is close to you, rather than a distant target.

2 Move around to the side of the ball and place your right foot in position while at the same time setting the head of the club behind the ball.

3 While checking that the clubface is correctly positioned on the ball-to-target line, bring the left foot into position.

4 Finally, check your grip is correct and your feet, hips and shoulder are all parallel.

Whenever you get the opportunity to practise, place a club parallel to your intended ball-to-target line. This will help you develop a better feel for correct alignment when you are out on the course.

The fundamentals of golf

Ball position

I've always thought that golf was a difficult enough game to master without trying to add further complications which, in my opinion, are not necessary. Throughout my career as a professional golfer, I have maintained that the position of the ball at address should always remain the same, regardless of the club you may be playing. When I set up to hit a shot, whether it is a driver or a sand wedge, I always position the ball forward in my stance at a spot just inside my left heel. It is vitally important that you establish the correct ball position as this is an integral part of your set-up and preparation for hitting shots. I believe that as I'm trying to make the same swing with every club, the ball should also be in the same position for every shot.

In this picture I am at the address position ready to hit my driver, with the ball positioned just inside my left heel.

The only two things that change in my set-up are the distance I stand from the ball with each club and the width of my stance. The different lengths of the shafts dictate that I stand further away from the ball with the driver than I do with the wedge. My stance with the driver is wider than it is with the wedge, because as the driver is the longest club in the bag it creates more swing momentum and I need a wider stance to help control my balance. The wedge, which is one of the shortest clubs in the bag, does not generate as much momentum and therefore I don't require a wide stance in order to keep my balance.

Once again at address, but this time about to hit a pitching wedge. As you can see, the ball is positioned in exactly the same place as it is for the driver.

The fundamentals of golf

Ball position

From my set-up position with the ball just inside my left heel, I can play every club in the bag, without having to move. The only alteration that I would make would be to narrow the width of my stance as I moved progressively down through the clubs from the driver to the sand wedge. I like to feel that I'm making the same swing with every club and having the ball positioned in the same place for each shot makes this easier to achieve.

Looking from head on, you can see how the ball is positioned just inside my left heel with all four clubs. In this picture my stance is fairly wide, as it would be for hitting the driver. However, when I come down to the wedge, my stance would be considerably narrower but the ball position would remain the same.

The fundamentals of golf

Swing plane

If you imagine that the golf swing is a wheel and that your head represents the hub of that wheel, then the swing plane is the angle on which the wheel turns around the hub. This angle is usually determined by the golfer's height and the length of the club being used. The swing plane will be flatter with the driver because the length of the shaft dictates that the golfer stands further from the ball. Likewise when the player moves closer to the ball to play a wedge shot, the shorter shaft will change the plane and the swing will become more upright. This alteration to the swing plane happens naturally as the body changes the angle of the spine by altering the posture to suit the different club lengths.

Bill has swung the club back too steeply and, as a result, he is out of plane when the club reaches the top of the backswing. This can happen for several reasons, the most common of which being a weak grip, poor posture and picking the club up too quickly in the backswing.

This picture demonstrates what happens when the hand action is delayed too long and the shoulder and arms take over. The club is pulled back low and inside the correct backswing path, producing a swing plane that is far too flat.

When the swing is operating within the correct plane, at the top of the backswing, a line drawn from the ball would run parallel up across the top of the left arm, the back of the left wrist, with the clubface also parallel to that line.

The fundamentals of golf

Posture

Good posture is one of the keys to hitting good shots because it plays a major role in both establishing and controlling the plane of the swing. Important factors such as balance, head position and weight distribution cannot be achieved consistently without good posture. Correct posture means that the weight is evenly distributed between both feet and over the balls of the feet, rather than back on the heels. The top half of the body should be angled forward but the back should be kept reasonably straight and not permitted to stoop over the ball. The legs should remain flexed and ready to help initiate the swing. Stiff legs at address can rob the swing of suppleness and rhythm. Good posture helps maintain the correct head position at the hub of the circle throughout the swing.

1 Bill demonstrates a common posture fault among newcomers to the game. The hands are a little too high, the legs too stiff and straight and the weight too much on the heels. If Bill initiated his backswing from this position, the chances are that the shoulders and arms would dominate the start of the backswing. And without the hands guiding the club, this would lead to a very flat swing plane.
2 Bill's poor posture has led to him stooping over the ball at address. This has the effect of pushing the hands down too far, with the result that the club is likely to be picked up far too steeply in the backswing and moves outside the correct swing plane.

As I take up my address position I'm concentrating on keeping my knees flexed and my weight evenly distributed between both feet. My hands are neither too low nor too high but in a good position as the result of correct posture. My head is still and my legs feel supple and ready to play an active part in my swing.

Practice and warm-up

There is no point in going to the practice tee and simply hitting balls. You should always have a purpose when you practise, and throughout my life as a tournament professional, I have always geared my practice sessions around the basic swing fundamentals. Once I've spent a few minutes loosening up the muscles, the first thing I do is place a club on the ground parallel to my intended target line. This helps me check my alignment which, as I've already pointed out, is vital. Sometimes I will also lay another club down, with the shaft running from just inside my right heel to the place in my stance where I position the ball. So many bad shots stem from faults in these two areas, therefore anything you can do to improve this aspect of your game will certainly pay dividends.

Once I have established that my alignment and ball position are correct, I then concentrate on my rhythm and balance, remembering to check my grip before each shot. You should never hit flat out, either on the practice ground or on the golf course. When I play I try never to hit at more than eighty per cent. That way I feel that I'm in control of the golf club; if I want to hit the ball further then I use a longer club. As a youngster, I used to keep my mind alert on the practice ground by imagining I was playing shots on some of the famous golf courses around the world. This exercise also helped me to develop the ability to visualize shots; something I feel all golfers should learn to do if they are to realise their full potential. Whatever ideas you might come up with to make your practice sessions both effective and enjoyable, remember to keep checking those swing fundamentals, over and over again.

Practice and warm-up

Don't make the mistake of walking onto the practice green and thinking that you have to immediately start holing every putt that you hit. All this does is put you under pressure and you lose sight of the purpose of your practice session which is to develop your feel for pace, distance and line.

Putting

When you are practising medium and long putts, work on developing a smooth stroke and try to get a feel for the way the ball comes off the face of the putter. One tip that might help you achieve this is to line up to the hole and place the putter behind the ball. Then instead of watching the ball, fix your eyes on the hole and hit the putt. You will be amazed how much feel you get putting this way. Don't be surprised if the ball starts dropping into the hole. A good tip for sharpening up your short putting is to make a ring of balls around the hole at a distance of approximately three feet. The object of the exercise is to move around the circle holing each ball in turn. If you miss one then you start again and carry on until you have holed all the balls. To help keep short putts on line and ensure that the club accelerates through the ball, I like to feel that I'm pushing the face of the putter through into the hole after the ball.

Don't fall into the trap of automatically reaching for your pitching wedge every time you find yourself a few yards short of the green. Look and see what the ground is like between you and the hole and if there are no obvious problems such as a bunker or mound which the ball has to carry over, you may get better results by using a less lofted club.

Chipping

Practise chipping with a variety of clubs to establish how much roll you will get with a five-iron as opposed to a wedge. The more you practise, the more confident you will become and the more options you will have for getting the ball close to the hole. The average club golfer misses more greens in regulation than he hits, so if you can improve your ability to get up and down in two from around the green, you could save quite a few shots per round.

This chart shows the degree of loft and the amount of roll you should expect when chipping with different clubs.

Wedge   33% roll

9 iron   50% roll

7 iron   66% roll

5 iron   75% roll

Because the club is usually swung on an artificially steep swing plane when playing from a bunker, you should finish off your practice session by hitting a few balls from the fairway to help re-establish your natural swing plane prior to playing.

Bunker practice

Providing that there is a practice bunker at your course, I would recommend that every golfer allocates at least twenty per cent of his practice session to improve his bunker play. From practice comes confidence, and this is the key to becoming a good bunker player. Start by playing normal bunker shots from a good lie. Then once you have found a nice smooth rhythm, spend some time experimenting with different types of lies and slopes. You should also vary the distance you hit bunker shots, as this will help you develop a feel for the different length and pace of swing required to carry the ball various distances. Set yourself goals, have fun and learn to enjoy the challenge of playing from bunkers.

Warm-up exercises

Many club golfers and newcomers to the game make a poor start to their round because they fail to warm-up the golfing muscles sufficiently prior to teeing off.

Ideally, you should arrive at the course at least 30 minutes if not longer, before you are due to play. This allows you sufficient time to hit some warm-up shots on the practice ground and also to spend five minutes on the putting green prior to starting your round or match.

However, if you arrive late at the course there are one or two quick warm-up exercises that only take a few minutes to carry out and which will help you get some of the kinks out of your body before you play.

The exercises that I am demonstrating not only help stretch the muscles but has the added bonus of simulating the action of the golf swing. Simply slip a club behind your back and lock it into position with your arms, then rotate your shoulders and hips as if you were making your normal backswing. Once you have stretched the muscles on your right side, transfer your weight back to the left side and turn the hips and shoulder through to the left in the follow through.

Remember to start gently, then gradually increase the amount of turn until your are fully stretching the muscles. Don't forget to bring your legs into the exercise by using them to transfer your weight back and through, just as you would with a normal swing.

From the tee

Too many club golfers rush onto the first tee without being properly prepared to play. They then try to smash the ball as hard and as far as they can and seem surprised when it misses the fairway and ends up in trouble. Take your time on the first tee and concentrate on putting the ball on the fairway, rather than into orbit, and you will have a far better chance of getting off to a good start. The opening hole on most golf courses is usually designed to provide a fairly gentle start, so take advantage of this by playing sensibly.

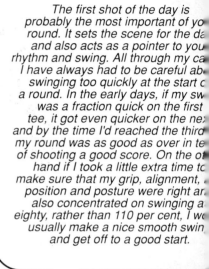

The first shot of the day is probably the most important of yo round. It sets the scene for the da and also acts as a pointer to you rhythm and swing. All through my ca I have always had to be careful ab swinging too quickly at the start c a round. In the early days, if my sw was a fraction quick on the first tee, it got even quicker on the ne and by the time I'd reached the third my round was as good as over in te of shooting a good score. On the ot hand if I took a little extra time to make sure that my grip, alignment, position and posture were right an also concentrated on swinging a eighty, rather than 110 per cent, I we usually make a nice smooth swin and get off to a good start.

- Never try to hit full out on your first shot of the day.

- Take time to check your alignment, grip, ball position and posture before you hit your opening shot.

- Don't be over-ambitious on the first hole — take your time and play yourself gradually into the rhythm you want to establish for the remainder of the round.

- If the opening hole happens to be a par four or even a par five, that doesn't mean that you should automatically use your driver.

- Make hitting the fairway your priority from the first tee.

Play every hole to your strengths and this applies even more so to the opening hole. Pick a target in the fairway that is well within your ability to reach, and concentrate on hitting the ball into that area. Repeat the procedure with your second shot.

From the tee

My swing

As a tournament player, I always felt that one of my best assets was confidence. I don't believe that players can make it to the very top without a total belief in their ability to succeed. However, confidence alone does not win Open Championships. It also requires a cool head, a steady nerve and a sound but simple swing. When I stood on the 18th tee at Royal Lytham, knowing that I needed to make a par four to win the 1969 Open Championship, I knew that this was probably the most important tee shot that I'd ever hit in my life. I was also aware of just how vital it was to keep everything as simple as possible and try to swing within myself. It's at times like this that you have to put your trust in the basic fundamentals and hope that your nerve will hold up long enough to allow you to make a good pass at the ball. Fortunately for me, it worked perfectly, and some twenty years later, I still practise those two excellent swing maxims: 'Keep it simple' and 'Play within yourself'.

2

1

3

1. Two keys to creating a good address position are correct alignment and a sound grip.

2. I always try to start my backswing low and slow, not forgetting the importance of keeping my head steady.

3. As the club reaches hip height in the backswing, my weight has now moved onto my right side and my left shoulder is starting to turn under my chin.

4. The shoulders continue to wind the upper part of my body as my head remains steady, which helps ensure that the club stays nicely in plane.

5. Here the shoulders continue to turn as I concentrate on keeping my head steady and my body balanced.

Notice how the position of my head has remained the same throughout the backswing. The head is the hub of the swing arc and therefore it must remain steady to ensure that the swing remains in the correct plane both on the backswing and the downswing. If the head is permitted to move up or down this has the effect of raising or lowering the swing arc and this can lead to shots being topped or skied.

From the tee

My swing

6 Shoulders have almost completed their turn with the left shoulder now directly under my chin.

7 As the club approaches the top of the backswing, note that my back is facing almost directly at the target and also how the back of my left wrist and face of the club are at the same angle.

This is the most dangerous point in the swing for the average club golfer. It is from here that many of them spoil any of the good work they may have done in getting into a good position at the top of the backswing, by rushing the downswing.

8 My left heel has been pulled up off the ground slightly, as the shoulders complete a full 90 degrees turn and my back is now pointing almost directly at the target. My backswing is still perfectly in plane and my head is in the same position as it was at address.

9 The first move in my downswing is made with my feet, rather than the shoulders, as I plant my left heel firmly back on the ground and start to move my weight back onto the left side.

10 No hint of the right shoulder coming into the downswing as the hips start to unwind and the club, still in plane, is pulled down with the left arm.

At this point in the downswing, many newcomers to the game would have started to hit at the ball, with the result that the wrists would have already uncocked and the right shoulder would have been clearly visible, coming round and over the top.

9

10

From the tee

My swing

11 & **12** With my weight now well established on the left side, my left leg remains firm and my head stays down and behind the ball. The hips continue to clear, allowing me to release the clubhead and swing through towards the target.

My swing is now completed; the club has reached a full follow-through position and my body is still perfectly balanced. One of the best tests of a well balanced and controlled golf swing is being able to hold your follow-through position after playing a full shot. There is no way you can achieve this by trying to hit at the ball as hard as you can. Only by keeping it simple and swinging within yourself, will you be able to achieve this balanced finish with any consistency.

Powering your swing

A question often asked by weekend golfers is: "How do tournament professionals hit the ball so far and straight, with so little apparent effort?" The answer, apart from a lifetime of practice and playing, is the combination of several factors, including: balance, rhythm, physical strength and good muscle co-ordination, all working together within an action controlled by sound swing fundamentals.

Strength alone is not sufficient, for although a strong individual may, through brute force, be able to generate distance, unless that strength is controlled and channelled in the proper manner, the chances of the ball travelling in the required direction are practically nil. Over the next few pages I will explain how power is generated and stored in the backswing and also the proper sequence in which it should be released in the downswing, in order to produce a shot which has both power and accuracy.

> The first move in the backswing is to start the club back from the ball with the hands, arms and shoulders all working together as a single unit. My head remains still and my weight is transferred across to the right side. As the club starts back, I am not thinking about how hard I want to hit the ball but rather how smoothly I want to swing the club. At this point the backswing is being controlled by the big muscles in my shoulders and back, as they start to coil the upper part of my body.

Many club golfers fall into the trap of snatching the club away from the ball with their hands. This prevents them from creating the necessary width in the backswing to allow them to swing the club on a shallow arc, something that is vital when playing long clubs such as the driver and fairway woods. The hands working independently in the backswing also encourage the hips to spin, rather than coil gradually as power is built up. And because the hands and hips have been too active in the early part of the backswing, proper weight transfer is not achieved. ▶

From the tee

As the club reaches shoulder height I begin to feel the large muscles in the left side of my body starting to stretch as the top half of my body winds against the bottom half. For although my weight is now fully transferred to my right side, my hips have so far remained square. My hands have also played a passive roll in the backswing until this point, but now the wrists start to cock as my shoulders continue to turn.

As the club approaches the top of the backswing, I feel my hips starting to be pulled around and the muscles in my left side becoming fully stretched. The spring is almost fully wound and there is a feeling of stored power, just waiting to be released in the downswing. My head has remained still and my left shoulder continues to turn.

Because they fail to create any coiling action in the backswing, due to the hands being allowed to snatch the club away too quickly, many newcomers to the game find themselves with most of their weight still on their left side as they approach this stage of the backswing. They also find their left shoulder starting to dip down towards the ball, rather than turning on a level plane.

It is because they fail to create a coiling action in the large muscles in the backswing that many golfers feel

The club reaches the top of the backswing; the shoulders have completed their winding action and the shaft of the club is now horizontal to the ground. The hips have been pulled round by the final stages of the shoulder turn and they in turn have pulled the left heel up off the ground. The left knee has also been pulled back behind the ball. The spring is now fully wound and the muscles are ready to be released in a recoiling action which will swing the club down through the ball and on towards the target.

The first movement of the downswing is to plant the left heel firmly back on the ground and transfer my weight back onto the right side. This is accomplished by making a strong lateral leg movement (towards the target). This thrust from the legs starts the shoulders unwinding and there is no conscious hand action in the swing at this point. The club starts back down as a reflex action initiated by the shoulder and leg movement, not as an independent action instigated by the hands and wrists.

they have to hit hard at the ball on the downswing, as a means of generating power in the shot. With their weight still mainly on the left side and the club swung back and up by the hands on too steep a plane, the only way back to the ball is sharply down. When the clubhead is rushed down at the ball from the top of the backswing, it causes the shoulder to spin to the left which, in turn, throws the clubhead outside the target line.

Golfers who hit at the ball, instead of swinging the club ▶

From the tee

Just after impact and the hands have now released the power generated and stored in the backswing at precisely the right moment to create maximum clubhead speed. The weight has been fully transferred to the left leg, which is now braced to resist the tremendous energy generated by centrifugal force in the through swing. The hips have been fully cleared to the left, allowing the arms to swing the clubhead down the target line.

Although the ball is now well on its way towards the target, my head has stayed back and my eyes are still fixed on the spot where the clubhead struck the ball. As the hips continue to unwind, the club is pulled on and upwards towards the follow through.

through towards the target, find it very difficult to keep their head behind the ball at this point in the swing. Because they leave most of their weight on the left side in the backswing, their efforts to hit hard at the ball in the downswing push the body ahead of the ball and they lose balance. Their steep out-to-in swing plane also pulls the clubface across the ball, instead of sweeping it down the target line on a slightly in-to-out path.

If club golfers thought more about their follow through

Power in the golf swing is generated by stretching the large muscles in the body to create a coiling action in the backswing. However, that power must also be delivered to the ball in a correct manner and this can only be achieved through a well-balanced and controlled downswing. As I complete the through swing, notice how my body is well balanced with the weight gathered on my left leg and my right knee pointing down the target line; something that would be virtually impossible if I was trying to hit flat out.

position before they started their backswing, it might help them get a better mental picture of the club swinging through a ball instead of hitting at it. If top professionals can't control the ball consistently when hitting flat out, what chance does the weekend player have?

If you are a newcomer to the game, I believe these two pictures are worth studying, because they demonstrate the means by which power is first generated in the swing and then later released in the through swing. The top picture shows the coiling action in the backswing which generates and stores the power, while the bottom frame demonstrates how the recoiling action of the downswing has accelerated the clubhead through impact and pulled it on to a full and well-balanced finish.

From the tee

A coiling action is created when there is a certain amount of resistance from the lower half of the body to the shoulders turning. This creates a feeling similar to a spring being wound. The further the shoulders turn, the tighter the spring becomes, before the hips are also pulled round as the club reaches the top of the backswing.

As the shoulders become fully wound, the action of the hips also being wound pulls the left heel up slightly off the ground. The large muscles are now fully stretched and ready to recoil into the downswing.

54

Footwork and coiling

The role played by the feet in the swing is important because without proper balance you will never be able to strike the ball consistently. The feet must play an active role in the swing to help withstand the pressure of the shoulders and hips winding as the legs take the body weight across to the left side in the backswing. An active foot action instigates the leg movement which starts the downswing, and the left foot must be planted firmly on the ground at the start of the downswing to help brace the left leg against the force of the body weight being transferred to the left side, and the right knee driving through towards the target in the through swing.

Having planted my left heel firmly back on the ground my next move will be to start to drive my legs laterally to the left.

From the two pictures above, you can clearly see the active role played by the feet, both in the backswing (top) and the through swing (above). The feet play an essential role by helping to balance the body throughout the swing and also assisting the weight transfer, both in the backswing and the downswing.

The backswing: low and slow

The first thing to remember is that you do not hit the ball with your backswing! Although the backswing does help in generating and storing power, its main role is to get the club into a position from where both speed and energy can be created, as the arms swing the club back down to the ball.

Unfortunately many weekend golfers fail to realise this simple fact and rush their backswing, destroying their rhythm and also losing control of the club, long before it starts back down to the ball.

Take your time and sweep the club away with your shoulders and arms, instead of snatching it back with your hands, especially when you are playing a wood or long iron.

The key things to remember when starting your backswing, especially when playing a wooden club or long iron, are to keep your head still and take the club away low and slow, at the same time allowing your weight to begin to move onto your right leg.

◄ In the first picture, Bill has started his backswing reasonably well but unfortunately he has allowed his head to move to the right along with the club. Moving the head slightly during the swing is not a major fault. However, if the golfer sways too far to the right, he is then forced to make a deliberate move to the left in the downswing to compensate. I have always felt that the golf swing is difficult enough to master without adding more complications and it takes great timing and considerable talent to make this additional move successfully.

In the second picture, Bill has cocked his wrists too ► soon in the backswing and now runs the risk of picking the club up too steeply. If this happens, instead of sweeping the ball off the tee from a shallow arc, the club will travel back to the ball on a steep angle and Bill could end up skying the shot.

I like to feel that my body is alert but relaxed, as I start the club back from the ball, I concentrate on turning my shoulders and keeping my left arm straight, in order to create a wide arc in the backswing. Creating this wide arc will allow me to swing through the ball on a shallow plane in the downswing, helping me to sweep the ball away off the tee rather than hitting down on it.

At the top of the backswing, my legs have transferred my weight onto the right side, the shoulders are fully coiled and my left knee has been pulled back behind the ball. From this position I am ideally placed to drive the legs back to the left and bring the big muscles into play in the downswing.

Notice how this picture gives the impression of my body being coiled behind the ball with the power generated in the back-swing, stored and ready to be released into the back of the ball. My knees are level, which will allow me to drive my legs to the left to initiate the downswing without fear of dipping into the shot or coming up on it.

Weight transfer

Because they often lack a proper understanding of how the golf swing works, many newcomers to the game start off by using only the top half of their body to generate clubhead speed, with the hands, arms and shoulders being the main providers of power. They make the mistake of thinking they must hit at the ball, rather than swing the golf club through it, with the result that many develop a steep out-to-in swing path and chop down on most of their shots. However, the real power in the golf swing is generated by the big muscles of the body, and the legs play a crucial role, both in generating this power and also delivering it to the ball at exactly the right moment and in the correct manner.

The main role of the legs in the golf swing is to transfer the weight from the left side at address to the right side in the backswing, and then back to the left side again in the through swing. This action allows the full weight of the body, along with the large muscles, to be used to generate power, instead of merely employing the smaller muscles of the hands and arms. One of the most powerful movements in the swing is made by the legs as they transfer the weight from the left side, back to the right at the start of the downswing.

In the picture opposite, Bill has failed to transfer his weight onto his right side in the backswing and has simply allowed his hips to turn as he picked the club up steeply, instead of sweeping it back low from the ball. There is no feeling of body coil or stored power in this position and therefore the only way Bill can generate any speed in the downswing is through his shoulders and his hands. He will be unable to use his body weight to create power because if he moves further to the left from this position, he will only succeed in getting ahead of the ball, long before the clubface reaches it and any power generated by this movement will be wasted.

The first and most important movement in the downswing is to plant the left heel firmly down on the ground and start the body weight back onto the left side. Many high handicappers initiate the downswing with the top, rather than the bottom, half of the body, bringing their shoulders into play far too soon. This action inevitably throws the clubhead out of plane and leads to an out-to-in swing path back to the ball.

Starting the downswing

Anxiety is one of the main reasons why many weekend golfers have problems starting their downswing correctly. In their eagerness to hit at the ball, they jump the gun and rush the club down at the ball. The key to hitting consistently good shots is being able to control the club and this can only be achieved by swinging within yourself. A golfer who rushes the downswing, will never be properly in control of the club. Speed in the downswing must be generated smoothly up to, and past, the point of impact with the ball, if both distance and accuracy are to be achieved consistently.

This picture captures me just after the moment of impact and shows the clubhead swinging on down the target line. My weight is well established on the left side and my head has remained still and stayed behind the ball.

The picture below shows Bill just as the clubhead is approaching impact. The club is moving on an out-to-in swing path, which is the result of Bill trying to hit too hard at the ball with his upper body and this has forced the club outside the correct downswing path.

From the tee

Starting the downswing

By concentrating on transferring my weight back onto the left side as the first movement of the downswing, I have not permitted the shoulders and hands to dominate the swing at this vital stage. The club has started down perfectly in plane and there is no risk of the right shoulder coming over the top and forcing the club onto an out-to-in path.

Instead of making a strong lateral weight shift back to the left side, Bill has started to turn his hips to the left too soon as the result of his eagerness to get the clubhead back to the ball.

Because the clubhead is now travelling from out-to-in, Bill's arms are unable to swing the club along the correct path and the hands are brought in too soon in a forlorn effort to generate pace and power in the swing.

Because my action has been smooth and controlled, I have been able to bring all the essential elements of the downswing into play in the correct sequence; the weight is fully on my left side, the hips have cleared to the left, allowing the arms to swing the club on and through along the target line.

Instead of the club travelling on a slightly in-to-out path down the target line through impact, Bill has now been forced to swing the clubhead across the line from out-to-in, and the likely outcome of this shot would be a slice.

Bill's problems started when he rushed the start of his downswing and because he was trying to hit the ball hard rather than swing the club within himself, he was never in complete control of the club.

From the tee

Follow through

Golfers who believe that a follow through is not necessary because the swing is completed as soon as the clubhead makes contact with the ball, are sadly mistaken. And unless they change their thinking on this subject, they will never realise their full golfing potential. This kind of thinking leads to an action which puts the emphasis on hitting at, rather than swinging through, the ball. It can also create a short, steep backswing and a hurried downswing. And because there is so much emphasis on the hit, many golfers who swing the club in this way, come over the top in the downswing, which can lead to slicing the long clubs and pulling the short irons. Another fact worth considering if you 'hit' rather than 'swing' is that using this action actually causes the club to slow down rather than accelerate at impact.

Keeping the club travelling through after impact not only creates more clubhead speed, but also enables you to keep the clubhead on the target line longer to produce more accurate shots

The follow through is the natural completion of the swing and also an excellent check-point as to the quality of the shot that you have just played. Only through a full and well-balanced position, can you confirm that you have generated maximum power and that your weight has been properly to the left side, with the hips fully cleared and the right knee (see below) having driven through towards the target.

From the tee

Your swing and mine

There are many different ways of swinging a golf club; you only have to see the likes of Greg Norman and Lee Trevino in action to realise that. However, despite the many differences in the way they swing the club, Norman and Trevino have one vital factor in common and that is the ability to consistently deliver the clubhead to the ball with both power and accuracy. It doesn't matter how you swing the club back, just as long as it is returned to the ball along the correct target line with the power generated in the backswing released at the right time and in the proper way.

Many newcomers to the game get off to a poor start because they commit the cardinal sin of hitting at the ball, rather than swinging the club through it. Brute force is not the answer. The components required to build a good golf swing are: a sound grip, proper alignment and correct ball position, combined with rhythm, timing and balance. The only way that all these elements can be continued successfully is if the golfer swings within himself. Strength is only an asset when it complements the other aspects of the swing, rather than dominates them.

Over the next pages I will be comparing Bill's swing to mine in order to highlight the reasons why he suffers from a fault which also plagues the majority of weekend golfers.

Bill's address position is quite good, with the legs nicely flexed and the weight evenly distributed between both feet. He stands fractionally too far from the ball but this is not a major fault. The real problems start as he begins his backswing.

From the tee

Your swing
and mine

68

Instead of starting the club back along the target line, Bill has allowed his body to spin inside too quickly. Because he has also allowed the left heel to come up too far off the ground, the hips have moved too far to the right and there is a distinct lack of coiling, or winding action, of his body in the backswing.

From the tee

Your swing and mine

Because he has allowed his body to spin to the right in the backswing, rather than turn and wind, Bill now starts down by spinning his body to the left. This will have the effect of throwing the club outside the correct downswing plane. Compare Bill's position to mine at the start of the downswing; his club is already well outside, whereas I have remained in plane.

Because Bill's body is spinning to the left rather than unwinding through the impact area, the club is moving around his body on a very flat plane with the club finishing around his shoulders. Compare this with how my club is still travelling down the the target line.

From the tee

Your swing and mine

As the swing reaches completion, notice how flat Bill's follow through is compared to mine. The combination of the body spinning to the left and the flat swing plane through impact indicates that the clubface would have been travelling from out-to-in on the downswing, which is the classic symptom of a slice.

Common faults

In this section of the book I would like to deal with some of the most common faults in golf. Slicing, pulling, pushing, skying and topping are the main problems that most weekend golfers suffer from at one time or another, not to mention the dreaded shank. Without exception, the cause of all the faults that I have mentioned, and many more, can be traced to failing to conform to one or more of the basic swing fundamentals. By learning these fundamentals and checking them on a regular basis, you will be able to avoid many of the common swing faults and also correct any problems that might arise in your game

Shanking

This is the fault that no golfer likes to talk about, for fear of passing on the disease to a fellow player! Once you've hit a shank you are always wary that it will happen again. Unfortunately, the more you worry about shanking, the more likely you are to repeat it. And with some unfortunate golfers, once they hit a shank they just can't seem to stop. A shank happens when the ball strikes the hozel, or neck of the club, rather than the face. And instead of travelling along the intended target line, the ball flies off at a sharp angle to the right.

Fear and anxiety are the main reasons for shanking and the problem usually arises when the golfer is attempting to play a delicate shot. In this type of situation the player often tries too hard to get the ball close to the hole and attempts to steer the ball towards the target, rather than swinging the club freely. Anxiety also leads to the golfer allowing his head to come up too quickly in his eagerness to see the result of the shot. As the head comes up, it moves the body forward too soon and instead of the ball contacting the club-face it strikes the hozel and flies off to the right.

The cure for shanking is to concentrate on keeping the head still and making a proper shoulder turn. Don't grip too tightly and let the club swing freely, instead of trying to steer the shot. And it's also a good idea not to let your weight get too far towards your toes at address, as it can shift forward as you swing and contribute to hitting a shank.

On this occasion, Bill has been a little anxious to see where the ball has gone and as a result he has become tense and tried to steer the shot, rather than allowing the club to swing freely through the ball. He started the club back reasonably well in plane but when anxiety took over, he tried to steer the shot. This took the club outside the correct swing plane in the downswing and led to the ball striking the hozel rather than the middle of the clubface.

TARGET LINE

Common faults

Bill has managed to get the ball out of the bunker, but it has barely reached the putting surface, leaving him well short of the hole and faced with a very long putt to save his par. The reason his shot came up well short of the hole is because Bill committed the cardinal sin of bunker play, which is to hit and stop, rather than sliding the club under the ball and making sure that he followed through.

Bunkers

I know that many club golfers find bunker play one of the most difficult aspects of the game to master. On the other hand, tournament professionals would prefer to play a recovery shot from the sand rather than the rough or deep grass around the green. This is because the pros spend hours practising bunker shots and, by doing so, develop a knowledge of exactly how the ball will react when played from the sand. From practice comes knowledge; knowledge breeds confidence; and confidence is the key to becoming a good bunker player.

Common faults

Making a good shoulder turn will help you to avoid swaying off the ball in the backswing. Bill, pictured above, has moved too far off the ball at the start of his backswing, rather than turning his shoulders under his chin and concentrating on keeping his head steady.

Poor shoulder turn

The role of the shoulders in the swing is something that many high-handicap golfers fail to understand properly. Some see the shoulders as the sole source of power in the swing and, as a result, usually become slicers for life. It's true that the shoulders create power in the golf swing. By turning, they help to generate and store energy in other muscles such as the legs, but they should not contribute direct force to striking the golf ball.

Hitting at the ball with the shoulders can lead to the clubhead being thrown outside the correct swing plane in the downswing. This in turn causes the clubface to travel across the target line from out-to-in at impact, causing the ball to slice if the clubface is left open. If the clubface is squared, the ball is pulled to the left. To help prevent the shoulders from dominating your swing, try keeping your head steady and thinking of the start of the downswing more in terms of pulling the club down, rather than hitting at the ball. It is also important when it comes to accuracy, to check your shoulders are correctly aligned with your hips and feet.

Getting ahead of the ball

This is another symptom of hitting at, rather than swinging the club through, the ball. This often happens when players are faced with a long shot and, in their anxiety to generate power, they rush the downswing, starting the upper body moving forward before the club has started down. This excessive body movement produces exactly the opposite to what the golfer is trying to achieve. For not only does it rob the shot of power, because the arc of the swing has moved out of position, the downswing will now be too steep and the clubface closed at impact, resulting more often than not in a smothered shot.

Never rush your swing; the longer the shot, the smoother you should try to swing. Remember to check those swing fundamentals, especially your grip and ball position. Make sure you take enough club and keep the clubhead travelling through towards the target on the follow through.

Common faults

The first thing to check is your grip, making sure that the V's point more towards your right shoulder than your chin. Next check your alignment to ensure that you are not aiming too far left of the target. Keep the thought in your mind that the clubface controls the flight of the ball. Try to picture it striking the ball along a square, rather than an open path.

You can see that as I start my downswing, the club is travelling on a slightly in-to-out path that will allow the right shoulder to rotate properly under my chin. Bill, on the other hand, has let his right shoulder get outside the line in the downswing and is now on the classic slicer's path, which will direct the clubface across the ball at impact.

Slicing

This is the shot that plagues around 90 per cent of club golfers, and it is caused mainly by breaking three of the basic swing fundamentals; two of which can almost certainly be spotted before the slicer even starts his swing. The first fault is usually a 'weak' grip, with the hands turned too far to the left. The second problem normally stems from poor alignment, with the body aiming well to the left of the intended target line. The combination of a weak grip and poor alignment leads to the club going back outside the ball-to-target line. The only way the golfer can get back to the ball is to come over the top with the right shoulder in the downswing, forcing the club onto an out-to-in plane which pulls the clubface across the ball at impact, imparting right-to-left sidespin.

And to further compound his problems, when playing a hole with trouble on the right, the slicer will aim even further off to the left, in order to compensate for his slice. Unfortunately the further left he aims, the more sidespin he will apply to the ball resulting in an even bigger slice.

The slicer's grip, with the hands in a weak position through being turned too far to the left. (Above) This shows the position of the back of the left wrist square to the swing plane at the top of the backswing. (Below) This shows the wrists open, or cupped, at the top. This is a perfectly acceptable position if you hit the ball reasonably straight, but it could cause problems if you are a habitual slicer.

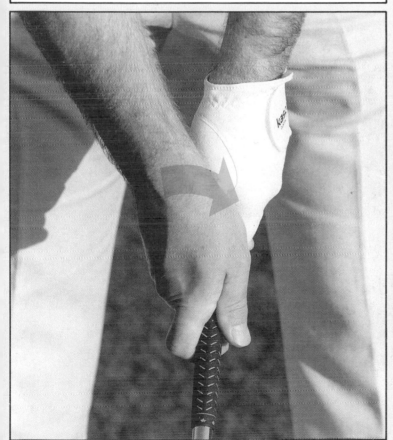

When the grip is too strong, the wrists often assume an arched position at the top of the backswing, with the clubface appearing closed. A hook is often, the result of too much right-side dominance in the swing, therefore make sure that your shoulders are square to the target line at address and make a conscious effort to swing the club through towards the target in the downswing.

Hooking

A hook occurs as the result of the clubhead crossing the ball-to-target line on an in-to-out swing path, with the clubface closed at impact. This action imparts an anti-clockwise spin on the ball, causing it to curve to the left. Fewer golfers hook than slice but nevertheless both tend to make the same mistake when attempting to cure their problem. Whereas the slicer aims further left to compensate for his slice, the hooker aims further to the right to accommodate his hook — the outcome is usually even bigger slices and hooks.

As with most swing problems, the cure can usually be found in the basic swing fundamentals of grip, alignment and ball position. In the case of both slicing and hooking, it is also important to check that you align the clubface square to the target and that the clubhead sits flat on the ground at address. If the heel of the club is touching the ground and the toe is well off the ground, the heel will contact the ground first at impact, twisting the clubface to the left, as it makes contact with the ball.

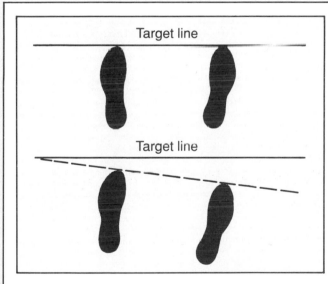

The most common reason for hooking is using too strong a grip with the hands turned too far to the right. Instead of the V's formed by the thumb and forefingers pointing between the chin and the left shoulder, they are pointing well outside the right shoulder. With a normal grip, when the golfer looks down he should be able to see between two and two-and-a-half knuckles showing on his left hand. When the grip is too strong, the number of knuckles on view would be at least three, perhaps even four.

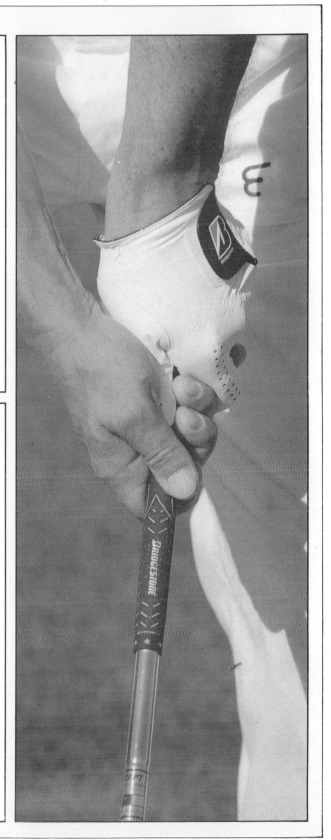

Common faults

Chipping

Chipping from around the green is the area of the game that professional golfers spend more time working on than any other. They too can miss greens, but if you can become proficient at getting the ball up and down in two shots, it not only saves shots but also takes the pressure off your long game. When you watch the likes of Seve Ballesteros or Ian Woosnam consistently get the ball close to the hole from just short of the putting surface, believe me it's not luck. It's the result of hundreds of hours of practice, developing the feel and touch required to play this type of shot well.

1 At address I'm relaxed with my knees comfortably flexed and, as you can see, I'm also gripping well down the handle for maximum control of the club.
2 Keeping my head absolutely still, I've taken the club back at a steep angle and slightly on the outside.
3 The club has come down from slightly outside the target line and slid under the ball, lifting it up quickly. However, although the ball is well on its way to the hole, my head is still in the same position.

One of the main reasons why high handicappers fail to get up and down regularly is because they line up incorrectly. The stance should be open with the hands positioned slightly ahead. The ball is positioned well forward in the stance and the weight is kept mainly on the left side. These four factors all encourage the club to move back outside the target line and create the steep angle of attack back to the ball which permits the golfer to swing the club down consistently on the same out-to-in swing plane.

4 Although the shot I'm playing is comparatively short, I have still kept the club swinging through towards the target and not permitted the right hand to cross over the left.

5 Bill, through taking the club back too much on the inside, has returned to the ball on a very shallow arc and instead of floating the shot gently towards the hole he has stabbed the club into the ground, leaving the ball well short of the hole.

Common faults

Topping often happens when the golfer becomes tense, usually because he is facing an important shot. Try not to think about the outcome of the shot but instead make sure you have taken enough club and concentrate on making a smooth swing.

Keep your head still and try not to tense up during the swing. It will also help if you concentrate on making a smooth swing and ensure that you also get your weight back across to the left side at the start of the downswing.

Topping

Topping is one of the most common faults among newcomers to the game. Instead of contacting the ball at the lowest point of the downswing the clubhead is in fact moving up when it meets the ball. The result is that instead of being compressed into the turf by the full face of the club, the ball is struck with the leading edge of the clubface and never gets off the ground.

Skying

Skying normally happens with the driver or wooden clubs, because the golfer chops down on the ball on an out-to-in swing path, rather than sweeping it away off the tee from a slightly in-to-out path. As with most faults, the cure can usually be found by checking the swing fundamentals. Make sure that at address, the ball is in the correct position opposite the left heel, check that your grip is not too strong and don't permit the wrists to cock too early in the backswing.

Bill has picked the club up too steeply in the backswing and as a result he has failed to transfer his weight properly onto the right side. From this position, he is almost certain to chop down on the ball from his steep out-to-in plane, instead of sweeping it away off the tee with the clubhead travelling through impact on a shallow plane.

From the fairway

Only from the fairway are you guaranteed a reasonable line and normally, a fairly level stance. Therefore any time you play from this position it is important to take advantage of these factors in order to put your next shot as close to the hole as possible.

Fairway woods

The fairway woods can be among the most helpful clubs in the bag for weekend players, provided that they learn to play them correctly. In fact, I would recommend that high-handicap players and those new to the game, leave the two and three irons in their locker for a while and at this early stage of their golfing development, concentrate more on becoming proficient with the three, four and five woods. One of the great benefits to be gained from these clubs is the way in which they can provide length and height — both are assets when it comes to playing long par three holes where the ball is required not only to carry all the way to the green, but also stop quickly on landing.

1 The set-up for the fairway woods is the same as for the driver, with the ball positioned just inside the left heel.
2 The club should start back low and slow from the ball.
3 Don't break the wrists too soon in the backswing but instead concentrate on keeping the swing arc as wide as possible.

The key thought in your mind when playing the fairway woods should be to sweep the ball away off the surface of the grass. In order to achieve this, make sure you don't pick the club up too steeply in the backswing. Keep your head steady and be conscious of trying to make a good shoulder turn.

One of the most common faults among high handicappers when playing fairway woods is topping. This often happens because they tend to focus their attention on the top rather than the back of the ball. Another problem is skying, or ballooning the ball. This usually occurs because the golfer tries to hit down on the ball in an attempt to force it up into the air. It also happens when the player fails to make a proper shoulder turn in the backswing, which leads to the club being swung back too steeply.

From the fairway

Hitting a good long iron shot is one of the most satisfying feelings in golf, and as long as you remember the basic swing fundamentals, there is no reason why you should not become a competent long iron player. One thought worth keeping in mind when you play a long iron is to imagine that you have a seven iron in your hand. Try to swing the club with the same unhurried pace and smooth rhythm that you would adopt with the shorter club, rather than thinking the priority is to hit the ball hard

Long irons

The long irons are the most difficult clubs to master for two reasons. The first is that because there is very little loft on the face, the club will produce less spin, making it harder to get the ball airborne. Secondly, these clubs have fairly long shafts which make them more difficult for the higher-handicap player to control. One of the other problems that arises from the lack of loft on the long irons, is that sidespin has a greater effect on the ball and this tends to exaggerate sliced and hooked shots. However, as with the fairway woods, the key to hitting long irons well is to make a wide backswing, a full shoulder turn and not to rush the downswing.

This sequence shows me through impact with a long iron. Notice from the follow-through position how I've maintained my balance — something that would be impossible if I was trying to hit the ball very hard. The pace of my swing with a one iron is the same as with a nine, which is one of the keys to playing long irons well.

From the fairway

Middle irons

The five, six and seven comprise the middle irons and are also the clubs that should be among the easiest to hit. Because the shafts on these clubs are considerably shorter than either the fairway woods and the long irons, they are easier to control. And as the faces on the middle iron clubs are also deeper, sidespin has less effect, and that will also help produce more accurate shots. It is important to know how far you hit all of your clubs and this applies especially to the middle irons. These are the clubs that, more often than not, you will be playing for your second shots to the par four holes. Knowing the difference between how far you hit your seven iron as opposed to your six, can mean the difference between your ball landing in the bunker short of the green, or finishing close to the flag leaving you a putt for a birdie.

As you can see from this picture, my head has maintained its original address position and the coiling action of the shoulders is already starting to pull my hips around.

The secret to good middle iron play is to take plenty of club and try to swing well within yourself. If you try to hit the ball too hard then you will destroy both your rhythm and balance.

1 My weight is distributed evenly between my feet, allowing me to take the club back on a wide arc without being pulled off balance.

2 With my weight now on my right side, the arms are fully extended as the left shoulder turns under my chin.

3 The shoulders continue to wind the upper body until the club reaches the top of the backswing.

4 As you can see from this picture, my head has maintained its address position, and the full coiling action of the shoulders has pulled my left heel up slightly off the ground. The club may not have quite reached a position parallel to the ground at the top of the backswing. Nevertheless there is plenty of power now stored.

It is the legs and lower body which start the downswing and not the shoulders and arms. This helps ensure that the body weight is brought fully into play in the throughswing.

5 The first move of the downswing is to plant the left heel firmly back on the ground and transfer the weight back onto the left side of my body.

From the fairway

Middle irons

The key to crisp striking with the middle irons is to make sure the clubface is travelling down and through, contacting the ball first, then the turf. This action will not only promote a better strike but also helps apply backspin to the ball, making it stop more quickly when it lands.

7

6

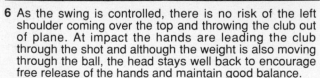

6 As the swing is controlled, there is no risk of the left shoulder coming over the top and throwing the club out of plane. At impact the hands are leading the club through the shot and although the weight is also moving through the ball, the head stays well back to encourage free release of the hands and maintain good balance.

8

7 Even though the ball is now well on its way towards the target, my head has stayed down and back.

8, 9, 10 Moving into the follow through and only now is the head starting to come up to follow the flight of the ball. As the swing reaches its completion, note how I have maintained good balance and how the head has stayed in the same position throughout the whole swing.

Notice how I have kept the club accelerating on to a full follow through at the end of the swing. If you compare this picture with the one which shows me at the follow through position after hitting a one iron (page 91) you will find them almost identical; which is as it should be, because I made the same swing with the middle iron as I did with the one iron.

This sequence shows me hitting a full wedge. Once you have taken up your address position, try not to think too much about the mechanics of actually playing the shot; rather allow the club to swing freely and ensure that you carry on to a full follow through. Because you are hitting the ball a relatively short distance, don't fall into the trap of using only your hands and arms to swing the club. The short irons, like any of the other clubs in the bag, should incorporate a good active leg action.

Short irons

The short irons are the scoring clubs. If you are playing well and hitting your tee shots long and straight, there will be many opportunities during the round to reap the benefits on your good play by hitting the short irons close to the hole. The shorter length of shaft and greater loft make these clubs easier to control. Sidespin will also be far less of a factor in the flight of the shot, which means the player can concentrate fully on judging distance and not be concerned about the ball slicing or hooking. Although the short irons are attacking clubs, many golfers still have problems producing consistent results. One of the reasons for this is because they tend to use a short swing. This is a mistake — to play the short irons correctly, you must make a full swing, using the same rhythm and tempo as you would when playing a medium iron or fairway wood.

The short irons are clubs that you should practise using. Not just because they can help improve your scoring but also because the heavier heads on these clubs can help you develop a feel for the rhythm and pace of the golf swing.

Getting out of trouble

Let's face it, there is no such thing as the perfect round of golf — where every drive splits the centre of the fairway, all of your approach shots find the heart of the green and every putt rolls unerringly into the centre of the cup. I've always felt that part of the challenge of this great game is learning to overcome the problems that come along when things don't go quite as planned. Pitting your skill, imagination and, on occasion, your courage against these problems, be they rough, bunkers, trees, awkward lies or the occasional bad bounce, is for me just one of the things that makes golf such an enjoyable and rewarding game to play.

Finding yourself in trouble does not automatically mean conceding that you will drop a shot. By learning the correct techniques and the right approach to playing from difficult situations, there are ways by which you can save par and, on a few occasions, turn what looked a certain bogey into a welcome birdie.

When playing from the rough, the most important factor is usually the lie, and most club golfers fail to play a good recovery shot because they attempt to hit a shot that is beyond their ability.

Learning to shape the flight of your shots can offer you a wider range of options when it comes to playing a successful recovery shot.

Shots that at first may seem impossible, can be played successfully, providing you adhere to the basic swing fundamentals and take a realistic view as to what you can expect to achieve from the position in which you find yourself.

The key to mastering these shots is to understand how the flight of the ball will be determined by the position from which you have to play.

Getting out of trouble

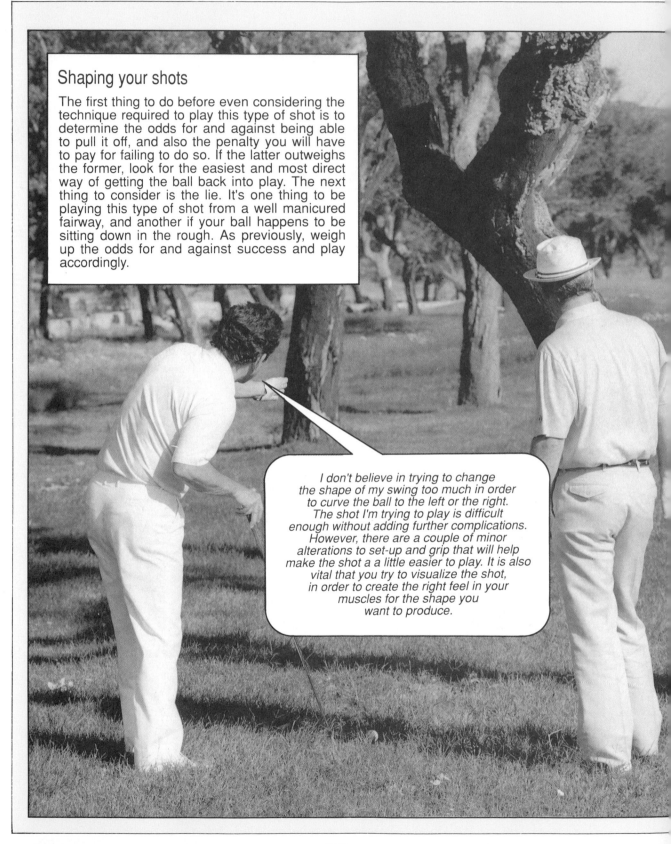

Shaping your shots

The first thing to do before even considering the technique required to play this type of shot is to determine the odds for and against being able to pull it off, and also the penalty you will have to pay for failing to do so. If the latter outweighs the former, look for the easiest and most direct way of getting the ball back into play. The next thing to consider is the lie. It's one thing to be playing this type of shot from a well manicured fairway, and another if your ball happens to be sitting down in the rough. As previously, weigh up the odds for and against success and play accordingly.

I don't believe in trying to change the shape of my swing too much in order to curve the ball to the left or the right. The shot I'm trying to play is difficult enough without adding further complications. However, there are a couple of minor alterations to set-up and grip that will help make the shot a a little easier to play. It is also vital that you try to visualize the shot, in order to create the right feel in your muscles for the shape you want to produce.

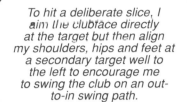

To hit a deliberate slice, I aim the clubface directly at the target but then align my shoulders, hips and feet at a secondary target well to the left to encourage me to swing the club on an out-to-in swing path.

I also weaken my grip and lower my hands a fraction at address to help pick the club up on a fairly steep plane, something which will also encourage the ball to move from left to right in flight.

With the clubface still pointing at the target, I would line up with my hips, shoulders and feet pointing well to the right. Whether hooking or slicing the ball, I prefer to make my normal swing and allow the adjustments which I've made to my grip and set-up, shape the flight of the shot.

If I decide that I want to hook the ball around the tree, then I would strengthen my grip to encourage me to take the club back on an in-to-out swing path.

Getting out of trouble

Awkward lies

I know that playing from an awkward lie is a very frustrating experience for most club golfers. On seaside courses in particular, there are many occasions when you can hit a perfectly good shot, only to find the ball has come to rest perched at an acute angle on some grassy mound, in a lie that appears to defy the laws of gravity. The key to playing these types of shots successfully is knowing how the flight of the ball will be affected by the severity of the slopes and different angles of lies from which you will be forced to swing the club.

As with hitting intentional hooks and slices, it's important to adhere as closely as possible to the basic swing fundamentals, even when you find it difficult to maintain your balance, let alone swing the golf club. Therefore the first thing you must do when playing from sloping lies is to set your body position as close to normal as possible.

It is important not to fight the slope, Instead adjust your body as much as possible to mirror the angle of the ground to enable you to swing the club as closely as possible to normal. And because the slope will affect the shape of shot you hit, this should be taken into consideration before you play.

All golfers, be they tournament professionals or rabbits, must compromise to some extent when it comes to playing from severe slopes. The secret is to make the slope work as much in your favour as possible, and that way, you may be able to turn a difficult lie into a rewarding shot.

Getting out of trouble

Awkward lies

At address, try to align your body as closely as possible to the slope without running the risk of losing your balance when you swing the club. The ball should be positioned further back in your stance to ensure that it is struck before the turf. Balance is critical, therefore don't attempt to make a full swing — settle instead for a three-quarter swing.

Downhill lies

This is one of the most difficult shots in golf to play successfully. The downslope will have the effect of de-lofting the club, which makes it extremely difficult to play a long iron. In fact, I would recommend that most club golfers never hit anything less than a five iron from a severe downslope. The good news, however, is that the ball will run further when it lands.

Uphill lies

The two biggest problems when it comes to playing from an uphill lie are trajectory and balance. The upslope will act like a launching pad, with the result that the ball is likely to fly much higher than it would from a level lie. Because of this, the ball will also stop much more quickly, something worth remembering when it comes to club selection. Because most of the weight is on the back foot at address, this makes it very difficult to get the weight onto the left side at impact. And if you are attempting to hit the ball a long way, there is a good chance that the shot will be pulled to the left. When you find yourself playing from a severe upslope it is vital to maintain your balance. Keep the knees flexed and try to mirror the slope as much as possible. Once again, position the ball more towards the centre of your stance. Don't try to hit the shot too hard; it is better to take one or even two clubs more than you need and then concentrate on making a smooth, well balanced pass at the ball.

Ball above the feet

One of the main things to remember when playing with your feet well below the level of the ball, is that you are almost certain to produce a shot that flies from right to left. It is important therefore to compensate for this by aiming well to the right of your intended target line at address.

> With this type of shot the arc of the swing is extremely shallow and the club feels as though it is turning around your waist. This shallow arc can cause the clubface to make contact with the ground before it reaches the ball. Therefore it's a good idea to grip down the handle of the club at address. This will not only help keep the spine as close to vertical as possible, but also give you more control over the club.

> Position your shoulders as far over the ball as possible without losing your balance and position the ball slightly forward in the stance. You will also find shoulder turn is limited, but don't make the mistake of trying to create power with your arms and shoulders alone. If you are playing a long to medium iron, select an imaginary target well to the left of the primary target and try to hit the ball towards it.

Ball below the feet

This is one of the most awkward lies of all and you should try to avoid the mistake of sitting back too much on your heels at address. As the legs will be almost totally occupied keeping the body balanced, the shot will require more hand action to compensate.

Getting out of trouble

The rough

The first rule of playing from the rough is to be realistic about what you can and cannot achieve in terms of distance and control over the shot. To a great extent, this depends on the type of lie you find, so take a careful look at the position your ball is in, before making any decision on club selection and the type of shot you want to make. The second rule of playing from the rough is to make certain, whatever shot you may decide to play, that your first priority is to get the ball back into play. From deep rough this should be your only priority.

It is important to get as little grass as possible between the blade of the club and the back of the ball at impact. It will help if you hold the club slightly off the ground at address as this will prevent the clubhead getting caught up in the grass at the start of the backswing. You must also take a firm hold on the club, especially with the last three fingers of the left hand.

Break the wrists early and swing the club back steeply to create the best angle of attack back down to the ball, without the head of the club having to cut through too much grass to make contact with the ball. Don't be afraid to hit down firmly on the ball. As long as the club you have selected has enough loft, you can hit down, confident that the ball will be forced up and out of the rough.

Don't take too lengthy a backswing. Keep your eye on the ball and a firm grip on the club as you drive it down and through behind the ball. If possible, also try to keep the clubhead going on towards your target after impact, although in very deep rough this may not be possible.

If you find yourself playing from really heavy rough, look for the shortest route back into play and use your sand wedge to play the shot. The short shaft length will encourage the upright swing plane required to get the clubhead down steeply into the back of the ball, and the heavy flange on the sole of the club will also add both loft and weight to the shot.

Getting out of trouble

The rough

One of the most common mistakes made by the weekend golfer when playing from the rough is trying to get too much distance from the recovery shot, regardless of the lie. Instead of accepting the fact that they may have to sacrifice a shot because of their error, many players attempt to make up for the original mistake by smashing the ball out of the rough and onto the green, regardless of both the type of lie and the distance the shot must travel to reach the putting surface.

The outcome of this type of strategy usually leaves the golfer playing the next shot from a few feet in front of where the previous shot finished, and usually still in the rough! However, landing in the rough does not automatically mean you will drop a shot. The most important factor to consider is the lie and if you know how the ball is likely to react when played from different lies in the rough, you might be able not only to save par, but perhaps even turn what looked like a certain bogey into a possible birdie.

Don't be afraid to use a fairway wood from the rough. Providing you have a good lie, it is often easier to hit a wood rather than a long iron. This is because the shape of the wooden head slides more easily through the long grass, while in the case of the long iron, the grass can wrap itself around the head of the club and twist the face off-line. If the ball is sitting up on a tuft in the rough, take care to set up with the clubface held above the ground. This will help to ensure that you contact the ball with the full face of the club, instead of risking the head of the club sliding under the ball.

When the ball is lying down in deep rough, the only objective must be to get it back onto the fairway by the shortest route possible. To ensure that you get the ball airborne as quickly as possible, play this shot as though it was a bunker shot. Using a sand wedge, pick the club up steeply in the backswing and then drive the clubhead down and through behind the ball, lifting both grass and ball out together.

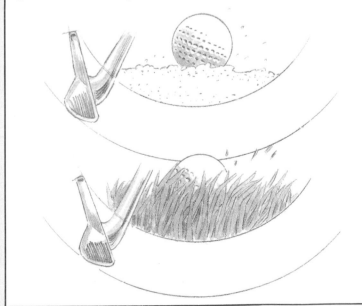

Playing from a divot hole

If you are forced to play from an old divot mark, the position in which the ball is lying will determine what you can expect to achieve from the shot. If the ball has come to rest at the start of the divot hole, it will be difficult to make contact with the bottom half of the ball. In this instance you may be forced to sacrifice distance and simply punch the ball forward with an eight or nine iron to make certain of getting the ball back into play. However, if the ball is lying close to the front of the divot hole, there is a better chance of making contact with the whole of the back of the ball and therefore you can approach the shot the same way as when playing a normal shot from the fairway.

Getting out of trouble

Bunkers

For many weekend golfers, the sight of their ball disappearing into a greenside or fairway bunker is the signal for panic to set in. For some golfers, many a good card has been ruined long before the end of the round, because of the player's failure to get the ball out of a bunker. Fear of failure is one of the main reasons for poor bunker play. However, by learning to use the club that was designed especially for the job and applying the same basic swing fundamentals employed when playing from the fairway, that fear can be overcome. Then instead of feeling apprehension every time he steps into a bunker, the golfer will relish the challenge of getting the ball back into play and trying to save his par, or make a birdie.

It is surprising what an hour or so in the practice bunker can do for your confidence, especially once you know the correct things to work on.

- Make sure your follow through is at least as long as your backswing.

- Address the ball with the clubface open and make sure that it remains open throughout the shot.

- Pick a spot approximately an inch-and-a-half behind the ball and concentrate on sliding the clubhead into the sand at that point.

- Keep your head still and don't rush your downswing; try to accelerate the club down and through the shot.

Getting out of trouble

> *One of the main differences when playing from a fairway bunker rather than the fairway, is that instead of hitting slightly down on the ball the golfer must attempt to pick the ball cleanly off the surface of the sand.*

Fairway bunkers

Most club golfers fear fairway bunkers because they automatically think that whenever their ball lands in one, it means they will drop at least one shot on the hole. However, providing that the ball is lying cleanly on the surface of the sand and the lip of the bunker is neither too steep nor too close, there is no reason why playing from a fairway bunker should be any more difficult than playing from the fairway.

> *Good balance is vital. Therefore you must work the feet firmly down into the sand to establish a firm base to swing from. Unlike a greenside bunker shot, which is played mainly with the hands and arms, the legs play a major role in the fairway bunker shot. If the feet slip at a critical moment in the downswing, the chances of getting any distance on the shot become fairly remote, and you might be lucky just to get the ball out of the bunker.*

> *From a slightly squarer stance, the backswing must be smooth and unhurried and the main thought in the downswing should be to try and pick the ball cleanly off the top of the sand or, at worst, contact the back of the ball before the sand. That way you may not reach the green but you should still get reasonable distance.*

Getting out of trouble

Greenside bunkers

As a youngster, I used to love practising my bunker shots. I relished the challenge of putting myself in difficult positions and then pretending that I had to get up and down in two in order to win the Open Championship. The following sequence shows the basic swing fundamentals which hold the key to improving your 'Sand Save' average from greenside bunkers.

The first thing I do when playing from a greenside bunker is to work my feet down into the sand in order to establish a firm base from which to play the shot. My stance is open and I'm aiming to the left of the target. The ball is positioned well forward in my stance and I start the club back on a steep swing path that takes it outside the line from ball to target.

The sand wedge was first introduced into the game by a great old American golfer and former US masters winner called Gene Sarazen. Until then bunker shots had been played with a variety of clubs, including 'blasters' and 'exploders', which were heavy old clubs that required considerable skill in controlling how deep the clubhead penetrated the sand when playing these shots.

What made the sand wedge so revolutionary was the

Although this is a comparatively short shot, notice the length of my backswing. My head has remained still and my eyes are fixed on a spot approximately an inch-and-a-half behind the ball where I want the club to enter the sand.

ad flange that was added to the sole of the club. This sured that the clubhead bounced through, rather than netrated, the sand.
As a result, bunker shots became much easier to

control and the sand wedge quickly established itself as one of the professional golfer's greatest allies. Modern innovations and further developments in design have made this club one of the easiest to play, providing you

Getting out of trouble

Greenside bunkers

Notice how I have swung the club down on an out-to-in path, which slides the clubhead into the sand and under the ball. You can also see that my right hand has not been permitted to turn over my left.

remember the basic swing principles of set-up, ball position and alignment.

Distance and trajectory are determined by the length of the swing and the depth at which the club passes through the sand. The biggest misconception among beginners when playing from a greenside bunker is the belief that because they are close to the green, they should only make a short swing. This is a mistake, for instead of

The ball is now well on its way towards the target but I continue to keep the club swinging on to a good follow-through position.

Plugged lies

If playing a normal bunker shot worries the newcomer to the game, finding his ball in a plugged lie must be the ultimate horror. This type of situation can happen for several reasons but normally occurs as the result of a shot played with a lofted iron, where the ball has landed in the sand from a very steep angle. Certainly, it's a more difficult shot to play than the conventional bunker shot but by making one or two simple adjustments to your address and alignment it can be mastered without too much difficulty.

The set-up for playing from a plugged lie is to stand slightly more square to the target. Instead of sliding the club through the sand on a fairly shallow level, this shot requires that the leading edge of the club be driven down behind the ball. Dig your feet firmly in to the sand and also set your hands more in front of the ball to encourage you to hit down firmly into the sand.

With this type of bunker shot there will be no backspin on the ball when it comes out of the sand and therefore it will run considerably further. Allow for this when you set up to play the shot. Don't get too greedy and try to get the ball stone dead from a plugged lie. If the pin is in a tight position it might be a more sensible idea to aim away from the hole and play to a safer part of the green.

Although the ball is partially buried, don't be tempted to shorten your backswing and try to hit the shot too hard. Your swing should be the same as when playing a normal bunker shot; long and smooth. Lead the downswing with your hands and try to follow through as far as you can, within the limitations imposed by your lie.

omoting a flowing action in the shot, it encourages the fer to jab down on the ball, with the result that the club netrates far too deeply into the sand, often leaving the ll still in the bunker.

On and around the greens

Although I may not totally agree with the old golfing adage which says; "You drive for show and putt for dough", a sharp short game and a smooth putting stroke are two assets that most tournament professionals would gladly trade a few yards from their tee shots to possess. At every professional tournament you will see the pros hard at work, practising chipping and putting, sometimes for hours at a time. The players work hard on their short game because they are aware they might miss one or two greens during the course of a round. However the ability to get up and down with a chip and a single putt can often get them out of a difficult situation and save their score, when some other part of their game is not quite firing on all cylinders. It is one of the ironies of golf that a three-foot putt has the same importance as a three hundred-yard drive because both count as one shot. And that is why it is so important to give just as much attention and care to holing a short putt, as you do to hitting a long drive.

Putting: The game within the game

On and around the greens

This is one of the most popular putting grips, with the forefinger of the right hand extended down the back of the shaft and the thumbs set parallel on top of the handle. Many golfers favour this grip because it helps to promote the feeling that the palm of the right hand and the back of the left are both pointing directly at the target.

The reverse overlap is the putting grip favoured by the majority of professional golfers. Here the index finger of the left hand is placed over the top of the last two fingers of the right hand. This allows the golfer to have all the fingers of the right hand on the handle, with both thumbs pointing directly down the centre of the shaft. The main benefit of using the reverse overlap grip is the way in which it promotes a strong feeling of the hands working together as a single unit.

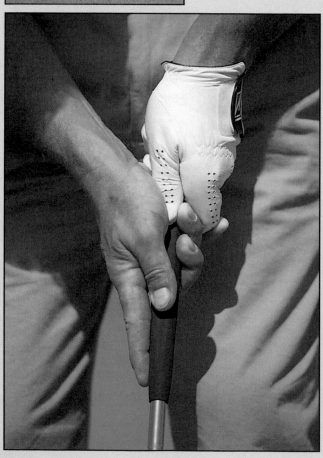

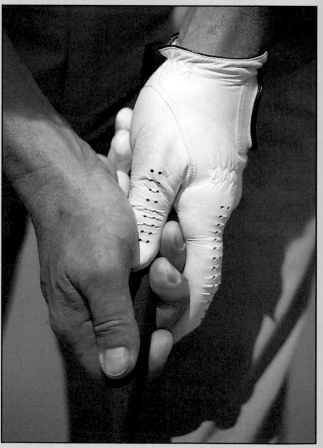

The putting grip

There is no right or wrong way to grip the putter. You can use whatever method you prefer, provided that it produces a smooth, repetitive and accurate action. The criteria for gripping the putter are the same as for all the clubs: to ensure that the hands work together and not as separate units. One of the main reasons for putting problems is tension, and when the golfer starts to feel pressure, this tension is transmitted to the hands, with the result that the player starts to grip the club too tightly. When this happens feel is lost, and putts that were finding the centre of the cup at the start of the round, begin to slip past the hole.

Whichever grip you decide to use, the hands must be positioned on the handle square to the target line. Once you have taken up your grip, you should be able to open the fingers of your right hand and find that the palm is pointing directly at the target. The same should also apply to the back of the left hand when you grip the putter.

This grip positions the right hand under the left on the handle of the putter and in recent years it has offered a life-line to golfers afflicted by the dreaded putting 'yips'. With the right hand placed under the left, the golfer has more control over the head of the putter, especially on short putts, which is the area where the yips are most likely to strike. The other grip (far left) is a further extension of the same grip and was also developed to fend off the yips. By anchoring the putter handle firmly against the left forearm, hand and wrist action can be virtually eliminated from the stroke.

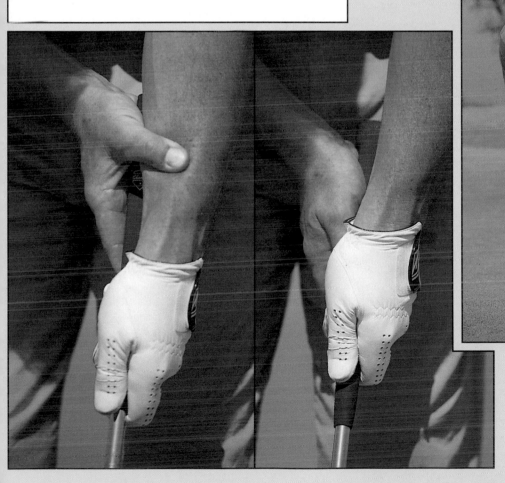

On and around the greens

An excellent practice drill for short putts is to circle the hole with five or six golf balls at a distance of approximately three feet, then move round the circle holing each ball in turn. If you miss a putt, go back to the beginning and start again. When you have holed all the balls in succession, move the circle back another foot from the hole and follow the same drill.

Don't wait until you get to the putting surface before you start to line up your putt. As you approach the green, look out for any obvious slopes that might give you a clue about the line of your putt. Try to get a general impression of the contours: Is the surface flat? Does it slope from front to back? Is the green soft or hard under foot? All this information can be gathered before you even reach your ball and could prove invaluable when it comes to working out both the line and speed of your putt. It is also worth remembering that when it comes to lining up a putt, your first impressions are usually correct. However, if there is any doubt in your mind, take a look at the line from the other side of the hole.

A tip that might help if you find that you are consistently leaving your putts short of the hole, is to hold the head of the club off the ground as you putt. This encourages the face of the putter to contact the ball on, or fractionally above, centre and imparts overspin, helping it to roll further without the need to strike the ball any harder.

Putting: the stroke

Two keys to good putting are keeping your head still and accelerating the club through impact.

In their eagerness to see if their putt is on line, many golfers actually move their heads before the club strikes the ball. This head movement inevitably leads to body movement which results in the club being pulled or pushed off line at the vital moment just prior to impact.

A good practice drill, especially when it comes to short putts, is to keep your head absolutely still until you hear the sound of the ball dropping into the cup. I also like to feel that I am pushing the head of the putter on towards the hole after it strikes the ball; this reminds me to keep the putter accelerating through impact.

Another excellent practice putting drill to quickly improve your feel for pace and distance is to putt while keeping your eyes fixed on the target and not the ball. Set-up in the normal way and having established that the face of the putter is square to your target line, fix your eyes on the target. Then swing the putter back and through, without ever taking your eyes off the target. Initially you may find your aim a fraction wayward, however once you gain some confidence, you will be amazed how much feel you can develop for both line and distance.

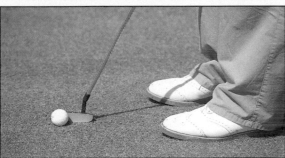

If you find yourself facing a fast downhill putt, line up with the ball positioned towards the toe of the putter rather than in the centre. Because the ball is not struck from the sweet spot at the centre of the club when you putt, it will not come off the face of the club quite so quickly, which means you will still be able to make a positive stroke, without fear of sending the ball miles past the hole.

On and around the greens

It is equally important in picking the correct line to judge the speed of a putt correctly. There is no point in starting the ball off on the right line, only to leave it six inches short of the hole. Equally frustrating is to hit the ball so hard that it fails to take the borrow and races several feet past the hole.

The art of putting is to be able to judge both pace and line correctly. And while the great putters in the game all have a natural talent for this, most golfers have to work hard at perfecting these skills.

Putting techniques are as varied as putting grips but you must ensure that the hands work in unison and that the face of the putter is travelling square to the target line when it strikes the back of the ball.

There are some golfers with exceptional feel and flair who can incorporate a considerable amount of hand action in their putting stroke. However, the majority of pros prefer to eliminate as much hand and wrist action as possible, especially on the medium and short length putts, and keep the hands and wrists firm, preferring to make stroke predominantly with the shoulders and arms.

To remove hand action from their putting stroke, many adopt a 'triangle' putting action, where the shoulders form the base of an inverted triangle and the hands become the point. Once the grip on the club and line of the putt are established, the hands are locked and the stroke is made by a rocking action of the shoulders. Some players prefer this because under pressure it is easier to control the large muscles in the shoulders than the small muscles in the hands.

Putting from the fringe

When the ball comes to rest against the grass on the fringe of the green, it can leave you facing an awkward shot because you are unable to ground the head of the putter behind the ball. If you attempt to use a putter in this situation, and fail to make clean contact with the ball, there is a good chance you will either top the putt, or stub the putter into the grass behind the ball. However, there is a way to play this shot successfully by using your wedge instead of your putter. Set-up with the ball in the middle of your stance and hold the head of the wedge fractionally above the grass, with the hands positioned directly above the ball to ensure that the leading edge of the wedge strikes the centre of the ball. Then, keeping the wrists firm, make your normal putting stroke.

An excellent practice putting drill to quickly improve your feel for pace and distance, is to putt while keeping your eyes fixed on the target and not the ball. Set-up in the normal way and having established that the face of the putter is square to your target line, fix your eyes on the target. Then swing the putter back and through without ever taking your eyes off the target. Initially you may find your aim a fraction wayward, however once you gain some confidence, you will be amazed how much feel you can develop for both line and distance.

Once again, keeping the head still is vital and you must also avoid stabbing down at the ball. If played correctly, the leading edge of the wedge will skim through the top of the grass and contact the ball on, or fractionally above, its centre. This will impart top-spin on the ball and encourage it to roll much better than if you were to strike down on it with a putter.

On and around the greens

One of the keys to putting well on greens with severe slopes is to pick a secondary target on the same side of the hole from which the ball will break. The distance that secondary target is from the hole should be equivalent to the amount of break you feel the ball will be required to take in order to drop into the cup. Having picked your target, ignore the hole and concentrate on starting the ball directly at that spot. If you judge the break correctly and also hit the putt at the right speed, the ball should start off at your second target. Then as the speed diminishes and the slope takes effect, it should start to turn in towards the hole.

Breaking putts

The main thing that distinguishes the truly great putter from the average putter is imagination — that ability to see in the mind's eye the line of a putt and be able to picture clearly the path the ball should follow to finish in the centre of the hole. Unfortunately, very few people are naturally blessed with this gift, and therefore the vast majority of golfers find reading the line on putts one of the most difficult and frustrating aspects of the game.

However, there are certain practical skills that can be developed to help improve your ability to read greens, but golfers must also learn to use their eyes when it comes to judging such things as speed and grain. Seaside courses, for example, are usually sown with a fine grass which produces a firm and fast surface. The average inland course, however, tends to be sown with a thicker grass and, as a result, the putting surfaces are usually softer and slower. In some countries, the grain of the grass is a major factor in deciding the line of the putt. In South Africa, for example, the grain is so prominent that it can actually change the direction of the ball, even to the extent where it will turn the ball uphill, seemingly defying gravity.

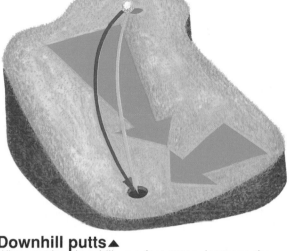

Downhill putts▲
When putting downhill on a fast green, increase the amount of break you think you will require. Because you will have to hit the putt softly, the ball will be travelling much slower than normal and therefore the slope will have a much greater influence on the line of the putt.

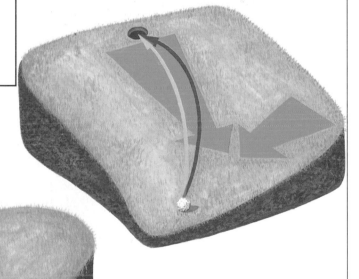

Uphill putts▶
When faced with an uphill putt, you should reduce the amount of break you think you require. Because the putt is uphill the stroke will be considerably firmer than normal, and therefore over the initial distance of the putt the ball will be travelling at a higher speed and the break will have less effect.

Sidehill putts▲
Judgement of pace is vital when putting across slopes. Therefore it is essential that you have a clear picture in your mind of how you want to hit the putt. If you decide to strike the ball firmly, then you should reduce the amount of borrow on the putt. If you prefer to have the ball 'die' gently into the cup, then allow for the maximum amount of break. In the case of short putts that have a degree of borrow, it is better to be positive than cautious. Most short putts are missed through golfers being too tentative and failing to hit the ball firmly into the hole.

Over the years, I have established that the clubs I chip best with are the seven iron, for low-running chip shots, and the pitching wedge, for higher shots. I suggest that you experiment either on the practice ground or even in the back garden to establish the two clubs that you feel most confident with and then stick with those clubs for all normal chip shots.

Chipping

If I had to recommend one particular aspect of the game that every club golfer should practise more than any other, it would be chipping. The average golfer probably misses as many as ten to twelve greens per round and on at least seventy per cent of those occasions, he also fails to chip the ball close enough to the hole to save par. It doesn't take a mathematical genius to work out just how many shots per round these players would save if they could improve their performance around the greens by only fifty per cent. There are also other advantages to be gained by becoming competent at getting up and down in two from around the green. For example, there is much less pressure on your approach play and because of this you will probably hit more shots closer to the hole.

Being a good chipper also offers more alternatives when it comes to playing long and difficult holes. Instead of being forced to hit a fairway wood or long iron approach shot in order to reach the green, you have the option of playing safe by laying up short of the green and then chipping and putting for your par. I can't emphasise enough the importance of practising this aspect of your game. It may not seem as exciting as smashing the ball miles with your driver. However, I can assure you that becoming a good chipper is one of the quickest ways I know to knock shots off your handicap.

On and around the greens

In an attempt to get the ball up quickly, Bill has stabbed down on the shot and although he did succeed in getting the ball airborne, the shot lacked any penetration and finished well short of the intended target. You must allow the club to swing freely and try to avoid steering the shot. For although there is a minimal amount of leg action required, the hands, wrists, arms and shoulder must all be permitted to function smoothly,

The lofted chip

The golfer is usually required to play this shot when there is a hazard such as a bunker, between the ball and a direct line to the hole. And because there is often a limited amount of space between the hazard and the hole in which to land the ball, this shot has to fly on a high trajectory to enable the ball to land softly with the minimum amount of roll. Many newcomers to the game find this shot difficult to play because they make the mistake of attempting to lift the ball into the air, instead of allowing the loft on the club to accomplish this for them. Instead of using a scaled-down version of the swing required to play a full shot, they either make a hurried stab at the ball or try to scoop it into the air, usually with disastrous results.

● Grip the club at the bottom of the handle to increase your feel for the shot. The closer you are to the ball, the more control you have over it.

● Try to put any thoughts of the hazard out of your mind and visualize the ball flying gently through the air and landing softly on the green.

● Keep your head still, accelerate the clubhead smoothly through the ball and carry on to a follow through which is at least as long as your backswing.

This shot can be played with either the wedge or the sand wedge, depending on the lie, how high the ball is required to fly and also how far the shot has to travel. Set-up with the ball well forward in the stance, your feet only a few inches apart and the weight favouring the left side. This not only encourages you to hit down and through the shot but also helps prevent swaying in the backswing.

On and around the greens

Chip and run

The biggest mistake most weekend golfers make when playing a chip and run shot is selecting the wrong club. As with any shot from around the green, club selection should be determined by the terrain between the ball and the hole. The closer you can keep the ball to the ground, the easier it is to judge distance. Generally speaking, the more lofted the club, the more difficult the shot, so I would not recommend using a wedge if the ground is reasonably flat between your ball and the hole. Ideally use a club that will carry the ball comfortably over the fringe grass and onto the putting surface, while still allowing sufficient distance for the ball to roll out and stop close to the hole centre and impart overspin, helping it to roll further, without the need to strike the ball any harder.

Before I play a chip and run shot, I pick a spot on the green where I want the ball to land. I usually play this shot with a seven iron and, from practice and past experience, I know if I can drop the ball on this spot. It should then run the rest of the way to the hole.

At address, the feet should be fairly close together, with the ball just to the right of centre. The hands are positioned ahead of the ball, with the back of the left hand facing the target.

The left hand should control the shot and the weight, which is mainly on the left side, should remain there throughout the shot.

The action employed is very similar to that used when hitting a long putt; the hands and wrists remain firm throughout the stroke, and the only major movement is made by the shoulders as they swing the club back and through. Don't be tempted to pick the club up with your right hand in the backswing because you are worried that the ball will not get up high enough to clear the longer grass around the fringe of the putting surface. There is more than enough loft on the club to fly the ball on to the green.

emember to keep your head still and don't rush the ot. Because you are using a fairly straight-faced club, en a gentle swing will be sufficient to send the ball a nsiderable distance.

The mind game

The mind game

One of the differences between the professional and the amateur can be seen in their attitudes to playing a difficult hole. The weekend golfer looks down the length of the hole and the first thing he sees are the hazards — trees, bunkers, water and out-of-bounds are the things that become uppermost in his mind as he steps up to play his shot. And the outcome more often than not is that the tee shot finishes up in one of the aforementioned places. Either that, or he is so inhibited by the apprehensive attitude that he has developed prior to playing his shot, that he barely makes contact with the ball and ends up topping his drive a few yards off the tee. The tournament professional, on the other hand, looks at the hole differently. He is aware of the hazards but will have worked out how he intends to play the hole and his attention will quickly focus on the area in the fairway that he has picked out as the place he would like his drive to finish.

This not only blocks out any negative thoughts about hazards but it also gives him a positive target to focus his mind on as he steps up to hit the tee shot. The golf course can be seen as a battle of wits, or a chess match, between the architect who designed the course and the golfer who plays on it. On certain holes the designer has built in hazards that are more psychological than physical and the golfer has to develop his own mental ploys to counter them. Over the years I've used one or two different ideas to help me mentally and one in particular stood me in good stead any time I found myself faced with a difficult driving hole. As I stood on the tee, instead of looking down the fairway, I would pick a spot in the far distance — a tree, a hill top, or even a cloud formation — and use that as my target. I'd line up on the object that I'd picked out and then try to hit the ball towards that spot.

The mind game

On short holes it is especially important that you have a positive picture in your mind of the shot you want to play. Indecision is a recipe for disaster, so keep that image in your mind as you set-up to hit your shot. Ignore any hazards that might be guarding the green; be positive and play the shot you want to play.

Short hole strategy

The par three holes are one of the keys to good scoring. If you can make threes or better at all of them, it will certainly make up for the odd shot dropped at one or two of the longer par fours. As I demonstrated earlier, any time you are hitting flat out you run the risk of producing a wayward shot. Yet when most weekend golfers step on to the tee at a long par three hole, they reach for an iron club, knowing full well that it will take a flat-out hit even to get close to the green, let alone near the flag. Four and five woods have become a godsend to the club golfer for playing these holes, because they provide height and distance without the golfer having to hit flat out to carry the ball to the putting surface. They also help stop the ball quickly when it lands. A long iron shot, unless you are a fairly accomplished golfer, usually has a low trajectory which means that hitting the green is one thing; stopping the ball on it is another. So much for the long par threes, now what about the shorter ones? On many occasions, especially during competitions, the flags are usually tucked away in difficult places such as behind bunkers or close to water. The golfer is tempted to go for the pin in the hope of making a birdie, but the outcome is all too often a bogey, or worse.

The problem is that the club golfer seldom has enough control over his swing or precise knowledge of exactly how far he hits each club, to take up the challenge. Any time the average golfer is playing from further than 150 yards, I would recommend that he forget about the flag and try to hit his shot into the centre of the green. Regardless of where the pin is situated, you will always have a chance of making a birdie from the middle of the green. And unless the putting surfaces are exceptionally large, you should be in good shape to make your par. I would give the same advice to golfers facing an approach shot of similar length on a par four hole, where the flag is in a difficult position.

Use the same approach in bad weather or windy conditions. There is little chance of the average golfer being able to carry the ball 200 yards into a strong wind to a green guarded by bunkers and water. My advice would be to abandon any idea of pulling off that one in a million shot. Instead, look for a spot short of the green that you feel you could reach relatively easily, which would leave you in a favourable position to chip and putt for your par.

Equipment

Equipment

To the tournament professional, golf clubs are the tools of his trade. That being the case, it is essential to the pro that these 'tools' are correctly designed for the job they are required to do and, when necessary, can also be adapted to suit certain physical playing requirements. Over the past decade, the development and design of golf clubs has accelerated at a tremendous pace with science and technology playing an ever increasing role in both design and manufacture. Golf ball development has also progressed at the same rapid rate and the modern-day golf ball is flying further, stopping faster and lasting longer than it did when I played regularly on the circuit.

However, perhaps the greatest leap forward in the evolution of the golf club has been in shafts. Here, space-age materials such as carbon fibre, developed in conjunction with computer-enhanced design facilities, have produced much more sophisticated equipment which can now provide consistently more accurate results. Shafts are now readily available in a wide range of flexes and step patterns, both for the tournament professional and the club golfer. Yet despite all the benefits offered by modern technology, many golfers are still playing with clubs totally unsuited to their requirements. Buying the most expensive clubs does not necessarily guarantee success, so before you decide to splash out on a new set, pay a visit to your local golf club and ask the professional for some advice. It is usually free and I'm sure that you will find it helpful.

The maximum number of clubs you are permitted to carry while playing in a competition is fourteen. In my case I carry a driver and three wood, one iron to sand wedge plus a putter. All the clubs in my bag have been tailored specifically to suit my swing requirements and this includes such things as swing weight, shaft flex, shaft length and even grip size. Also the loft and lie of the clubs have been set to suit my height and swing plane. As a professional golfer, I try to leave nothing to chance. The game of golf is difficult enough without adding the burden of playing with clubs that are not suited either to my swing or build. Having clubs tailored to suit your swing is something I would recommend to all golfers once they decide they want to play the game on a regular basis.

Equipment